The Simple Home

The Simple Home

The Luxury of Enough

Sarah Nettleton, AIA, and Frank Edgerton Martin

Photographs by Randy O'Rourke

The Taunton Press

The Taunton Press
Inspiration for hands-on living®

The Taunton Press, Inc., 63 South Main Street, PO Box 5506, Newtown, CT 06470-5506
e-mail: tp@taunton.com

Editor: Peter Chapman
Jacket/Cover design: Memo Productions, NY
Interior design and layout: Memo Productions, NY
Illustrator: Christine Erikson
Photographer: Randy O'Rourke, except where noted

The American Institute of Architects, founded in 1857, is a professional society of architects with over 70,000 members in the United States and abroad. Through its national, regional, state, and local components, the AIA works to achieve more humane built environments and higher standards of professionalism for architects through education, government advocacy, community redevelopment, and public outreach activities. AIA's website is located at aia.org.

AIA, The American Institute of Architects, and the AIA logo are registered trademarks and service marks of The American Institute of Architects.

THE AMERICAN INSTITUTE
OF ARCHITECTS

This book is published under the joint imprint of The American Institute of Architects and The Taunton Press, Inc.

Library of Congress Cataloging-in-Publication Data

Nettleton, Sarah.
  The simple home : the luxury of enough / Sarah Nettleton and Frank Edgerton Martin.
     p. cm.
  Includes bibliographical references and index.
  ISBN-13: 978-1-56158-831-2 (alk. paper)
  ISBN-10: 1-56158-831-8 (alk. paper)
  1. Architecture, Domestic--Psychological aspects. 2. Architecture--United States--20th century. 3. Architecture--United States--21st century. 4. Simplicity in architecture. I. Martin, Frank Edgerton. II. Title.
  NA7208
  720.01'9--dc22
                          2006019645

Printed in Singapore
10 9 8 7 6 5 4 3 2 1

The following manufacturers/names appearing in *The Simple Home* are trademarks: Rastra®, Trex®, Viking®, Zactique®

To all of you who are determined to simplify your life:

You know who you are. You can do it.

Acknowledgments

As with many things in life, writing a book—even a book about simple homes—is not that simple. Frank and I suspected that from the start, and in many ways it has been as complex a process as designing a simple home. A wonderful part of this complexity has been the collaboration among the many players on our team.

First of all, a big thank-you to the owners of the simple homes in this book for your willingness to help inspire others by sharing your homes and stories. Thank-you to the architects, for all the inspired answers you found to resolve design complexities into the essence of beautifully simple homes. Thank you, Frank Martin, for making my words poetic. And thank you, Randy O'Rourke, for seeing the simple beauty of these homes through your lens.

Finally, a thank-you to editor Peter Chapman, whose inspired behind-the-scenes guidance helped a couple of neophytes through the process of writing a book. You taught us to write in Tauntonese.

Contents

Introduction My first exposure to the simple life was during childhood summers spent at a Maine camp. Actually, that experience stretches the definition of *simple* to what my father called "studied inconvenience," meaning cooking on a woodstove and paddling a canoe to a neighboring camp for dinner. This simple home had no electricity and no road access. The luxury of simple meant that no man-made sounds drowned out the lap of waves or the trill of birds. In summer, a wooly blanket was all you needed to keep you tucked in bed at night, safe from the wilderness outside. As adults, many of us have forgotten such simple pleasures in exchange for temperature control at the touch of a dial and such assumed necessities as icemaker refrigerators and kitchen gadgets of every imaginable description. The pleasure of seeing a starry night sky on the way to bed is all too often left out.

The Simple Home is for people who crave a simpler lifestyle—not only in *how* they live, but also in *where* they live. In the pages that follow, we visit homes across the country where people considered the simple pleasures that give their lives joy and tranquility. The simple home is not an end in itself, but the means by which we can enjoy our own simple pleasures whether they be the starry skies that I remember from Maine or fresh air, gardening, or living in a place where you can walk everywhere. We spend so much time working and spending the money we earn that we have forgotten the basic pleasures of playing with a pet, laughing with our kids, or smelling the aromas of outdoor grilling.

Fresh air, fresh food, and clean water are simple, timeless pleasures that we all too often lose in our buy-the-latest-thing lifestyle. Yet, they are tangible and life-giving. This book doesn't give you blueprints for building a simple home. It's not a catalog of choices, but rather a collection of stories of people who found their own "studied inconveniences" and simple pleasures. The people we meet are young city families, single people, and retirees who didn't necessarily move "back to the land" to live off its fruits. Rather, they came home to themselves through a design process that considers their true daily needs and long-term goals.

Simple in this book describes design that is unadorned, resolved of complexity, essential in its response to needs, balanced, the result of clear choices, timeless as opposed to trendy. Simple homes achieve simplicity as a result of common sense, the wisdom of good choices, the elimination of nonessentials, and restraint. Whether large or small, traditional or utterly contemporary, the houses we visit are only part of the story. The true narrative is how the people who built them learned how to ask the right questions to find their own solutions.

Chapter One In Search of the Simple Home

In all the luxury of our comfortable, fast-paced life, something is missing. For many of us, it is the opportunity to come home and indulge in simplicity.

Cheryl grew up in a charming old village on the coast of Rhode Island. Yet, like many Americans, she left the small town of her youth for life in the big city. She lived for many years in New York, married, and had a son. Then, when the high cost of living and hectic pace of life proved enough, Cheryl and her family moved back to her hometown. They changed not only where they lived, but also how they lived. They built a new home for a modern family that fit into the historic scale and character of its shingle-style cottage neighbors (see the photo on the facing page).

Rather than going out to eat, they spend evenings at home cooking, reading, and playing outside. They found a way to simplify their lives by building a home that fits their budget yet is rich in gathering places, private nooks, and ocean views. Whether you live in the country, on an island, or in the big city, you can find a simple home that's right for you, too. Cheryl's story proves it can be done.

Why the Simple Home? Why Now? Many Americans long for a simpler life— and there are myriad books and guides to help us find it in daily routines and at work. Yet, most of us are unpracticed in describing to someone else (or even to ourselves) what a simple home for that life would really look like. We sense that something's missing in our hurried routine, but we have no idea where to begin the editing of complexity.

Scan the newspaper racks or the bookshelves, and you'd think we're living in a nation bent on attaining a simple, uncluttered, well-organized lifestyle. We are tempted to look for yet another gadget or closet organizer to simplify our lives—or a whole new house with ample room for everything. But when you take a look at the homes builders and developers are putting up all over the country, you'll experience a total disconnect between this search for a simpler lifestyle and the houses we're expected to live in. At the builders' home shows, you'll find gargantuan home theaters, the ubiquitous "bonus room," sweeping lawns to be watered and mowed, and kitchens with gadgets you'll never use.

What's wrong with this picture? If we crave a simpler lifestyle, we're not likely to find it in many of the houses being built today. The good news is that there are *some* houses recently built or renovated that espouse a simpler design and help their owners live a simpler lifestyle. What Cheryl did in her old beach town is one story of how a family found simplicity by design.

It's a story of asking different questions about where to live, the experiences that we value on a daily basis, and the home we need to shelter them. In this book, we embark on an exploration of 21 simple homes across the country and the experiences of the people who built them. These houses and their owners' journeys offer a fascinating counterpoint to the way most people buy new houses in the developer market today.

Defining the Simple Home Just what is a simple home? A Shaker cottage or a modernist white box might immediately spring to mind, but simplicity comes in many shapes and sizes—and the simple home can be defined in both tangible

and more general ways. Tangibles include a straightforward floor plan, a functional and unadorned interior, and abundant daylight. The rooms of a simple home typically serve many purposes and are flexible enough to change with their owners' needs over time.

Inside, the simple home is efficient and uncomplicated. Often intimate in feeling, it is light-filled, and its rooms serve many functions. The simple pleasures of natural light and ventilation are basic in the simple home. Human-scaled rooms are comfortable, even cozy, while still feeling spacious. The quality of spaces is often more important than the stuff we buy to decorate them. Often, a simple home has one color scheme throughout, with variations in different rooms. Plaster interior walls that enclose well-lit rooms rely on drama from sunlight and shadows rather than from fringed upholstery.

Simple design is practical and beautiful, like the rocking chairs, cabinets, and entire buildings once built by the Shakers. Shaker aesthetics provide a classic example of what we can do today in building and furnishing a home. They represent a labor-intensive investment with relatively inexpensive local materials—the very opposite of the $20 folding chair shipped all the way from China. Shaker and folk crafts come from an era when time was much more abundant than the money to buy and ship fancy materials. Today, we have many more options in materials, but we need to invest the time to craft our own environment, to be selective about what we buy and how much we really need.

Simple homes can also be high-tech, as we will see at a small new townhouse in San Francisco. We don't have to be mired in the nostalgic handwork of earlier centuries to find simplicity in life today. Today's fast-paced world offers vastly better communication, information availability, social diversity, and health care. Life, in many ways, is safer, more stimulating, and easier. We live in an abundant time, and we have many

more options in home design than existed even 50 years ago. How can we make the most of it?

In accordance with today's environmental challenges, simple design solutions are also sustainable. Using local stone, the simple home can quite literally be grounded in the region where you live. There's no long-distance transport required, with the associated costs of shipping, pollution, and petroleum consumed. From materials to location, a simple home is a part of its site and region, respectful of its neighbors and context. Its exterior materials are in harmony with its surroundings and do not call attention to themselves with bright colors or overscaled gables.

Whether the house is large or small, layouts and the placement of entries respond to contours so that all levels of the house feel connected to the outside. A new addition steps down the gently sloping site so that it's easy to walk outside no matter what room you're in. With simple sustainability, these homes take advantage of the opportunities of site in terms of light and natural airflow for warmer winter afternoons and cooler summer nights. Doorways are sited to take advantage of striking outward views so that in leaving home, you are greeted with a small delight every day.

Simple Home Traditions Simplicity in living and design is not a new idea. In traditions ranging from Christianity to Buddhism, letting go of the quest for wealth and possessions supports an inner focus, a calm, and ultimately a serene daily life. For many people today, freedom from desire offers far deeper comfort and security than the most lavish interiors and grand designs can ever provide.

Designing with just enough can lead to great beauty. For example, imagine a Japanese flower arrangement with just one blue iris and a few strands of spring grass resting in a tea-room nook. It's not the profusion of florid colors that matters, but the singularity of one bloom, the structure and textures of the grasses, the empty spaces between them that strike us. This simple arrangement is both luxurious and minimal at the same time.

In other words, simple homes reflect the wisdom of good choices and the elimination of nonessentials using the building technologies available today. They can be rich with warm woods, wall colors, door details, and fabrics. Yet, sometimes we confuse simplicity with a kind of monastic austerity or cold minimalism. Such extreme restraint is not right for everyone; nor is it always easy to maintain. If a glob of toothpaste on the counter wrecks the entire aesthetic of a bathroom, this space demands a lot of regular cleaning. If a living room is made visually cluttered by so much as a child's toy or a dropped newspaper, it will not be simple to keep ordered. Such self-conscious spaces call attention to themselves; they only complicate life.

Hallmarks of the Simple Home Regardless of style and setting, the simple home can simplify its owners' lives by offering the right amount of space in a functional arrangement. The following qualities are found in most simple homes:

- The floor plan and form are straightforward.
- Its style, be it modern or traditional, is timeless.
- Interiors are functional, human-scaled, uncomplicated, light filled, and open.
- Rooms serve more than one function.
- The design expresses a beauty in practicality.
- Siting and room layouts offer excellent natural light and ventilation.
- Details and finishes tend to be simple and unadorned.
- Storage is well located and often built in to minimize free standing furniture.

Pathways to the Simple Home The 21 houses that follow are organized into six pathways by which people have asked what *simple* truly means for them in both their lives and homes. Ranging from thrift to flexibility in design, these paths can help you consider your own home and how to simplify it. The paths are as follows:

• **Simple is enough** A simple house is a positive affirmation of "the luxury of enough." By this we mean that designing a simple home starts with figuring out how much you really need and what you can eliminate. The luxury of enough means confronting the fact that you really don't need an eight-burner stove and the larger kitchen to house it. Forty years ago, *utility* used to be a bad word in house design. In the 1950s rambler, the utility room was not exactly a showplace for guests. But today, many utilitarian buildings, such as warehouses and old barns, are very desirable locations for new housing and workspaces. They were designed for pure function for storage and industry, yet today they work brilliantly for open-plan living. They offer the luxury of space in a world of clutter.

Simple homes are often rectangular, sometimes square, and always "just enough," whether in terms of dormers, quantity of bathrooms, or square footage. In this pathway, we visit homes that reflect the way their owners choose to live rather than an image that they want to present to the street. These designs for "enough" appear deceptively simple because they actually grow out of a lot of careful decision making.

• **Simple is flexible** In simple homes, rooms are used in many ways. They serve multiple purposes. Think of an old farmhouse kitchen. Throughout the day and night, people gathered here. At noon, the farmer and the field hands ate their dinner. In the afternoon, the children studied by the warmth of the cookstove. In the evening, the family gathered

for supper. In this pathway, we visit a modern addition, a new house, and a small barn that express these qualities today, where kitchens are once again places for all-day activities such as entertaining, dining, and reading. Such multipurpose rooms work for a large gathering or for a cozy moment with a cup of tea. A simple space is a flexible stage for living rather than a straitjacket set of single-purpose rooms.

• **Simple is thrifty** Simple homes are often thrifty in both economic and ecological terms. In this pathway, we explore the efficiencies of open floor plans, expedient building massing, and a cost-saving central utilities core. In the houses we visit, thrifty design considers long-term "life-cycle" costs such as heating, cooling, and maintenance. It affords summer cross-ventilation rather than immense air-conditioning systems.

Simple thrift helps to make life in expensive places affordable. In Brooklyn, we visit a new infill townhouse designed with thrifty modern cement-board siding that complements a 19th-century rowhouse district. From inside and out, it's a clearly modern place, but it also fits into the neighborhood and the contemporary lives of the parents and kids who live there. Respecting the historic context of its neighbors, this simple row house is an affordable solution to having a home, a yard, and even a garage in one of the most expensive cities in the world.

• **Simple is timeless** Because simple homes are not about impressing other people or keeping up with fashion, they tend to be timeless. They can be folk-vernacular, like a New Mexico adobe; informal, like a beach house in Florida; or even very modern, like a corrugated metal-clad cabin in Washington State. Simple homes are not designed with a single style or size. Their owners ask timeless questions in the process of designing them, questions that address the local landscape, how much space they really need, and how they want to

socialize. Simple homes answer these questions with lasting materials and direct solutions, such as well-proportioned hallways and living rooms rather than the trumpery of decoration and nonfunctional dormers, archways, and gables.

• **Simple is sustainable** Sustainability is a trendy architectural idea that has actually been part of residential construction for thousands of years. Simple homes and sustainable design are often the same thing. In this pathway, we explore simple daylight, siting, and ventilation strategies that are available to everyone. You do not need advanced technologies or expensive products to achieve the spirit of sustainable design.

On the South Side of Chicago and the North Shore of Lake Superior, we visit houses that make the best use of today's sustainable building materials and mechanical systems to reduce energy consumption and waste in an old front-porch neighborhood. Whether in the woods or on the street corner, we find that sustainable design practices are really grounded in common sense, and there are reasons to pursue them no matter where you live.

• **Simple is resolved complexity** Simple design gets to the essence of things, whether they are local building materials, the landscape where you live, or your family's daily routine. The simple home resolves seemingly complex needs and desires into a well-refined vision for the spaces you will need based on how you use them. The houses in this section tell stories of people who found that they needed less space and fewer rooms than they ever thought possible. The result is that the simple home becomes a tailored glove that fits so well you forget it's there. Living there ultimately involves less upkeep, less stress, and more time for other things.

Honesty in Building In all of these six pathways, we consider "simple" not as a style of home design but as an approach to building a home marked by honesty and careful choices. Simple homes are, above all, authentic. They make no pretensions. More important than size, cost, or style, the simple house says what it is; it expresses the carefully considered needs and tastes of the people who live there. It is not designed to please someone else.

People today are creating simple homes that may be modern or evocative of historic roots. Yet, they are not designed for curb appeal or to create a stage-set picture of a mythic past. Regardless of size or style, simple homes are true to the people who build them, their sites, and the realities and opportunities of construction technology today. And they are as different as the people who build them.

In upstate New York, we meet a painter who found a humble farmhouse and renovated it while preserving its soul. In New Mexico, we visit a couple from Michigan who built a new home in the tradition of timeless adobes. In San Francisco, we tour a new modern townhouse that takes in city and bay views from a tiny footprint. In each of these disparate places, there are no cascades of gabled roof peaks or thin veneers of brick to enrich the street façade. They are what they are.

The Simple Home That's Right for You How can you find the simple home that's right for you? In many of the houses that we visit, the owners relate how they learned something about themselves in the design process. A family in Tennessee found that less space can be better space. A woman in New England found that she didn't need all the couches she had lived with for years.

Part of building the simple home is learning what matters for you and your family and skipping the temptation to add costly options that you may not really need. Basics such as sunlight have a universal appeal across time and culture, yet we have lost sight of how to have natural daylight in our

homes. Instead, granite counters seem to be a must-have item even though their cost, a $10,000 up-charge, would go a long way to imbue a house with daylight. Why is this? Quite simply, it is easier to add on a "feature" than to spend the time designing a house to be an intelligent partner with the sun. The lesson is that building a simple home is really not about sudden inspiration or buying into the ideas of others. It's not a composite product that we can attain only if we assemble the right kind of furniture, clothing, and kitchens.

Simple Homes Embrace Future Possibilities In planning for your simple home, it makes sense to consider not only how you and your family live today, but how you will be living in five years, in ten years, or when you retire. As an expression of who we are, the simple home should also be a place to ponder who we can be.

Certainly, there are other paths to a simpler and happier life, such as cooking, spirituality, artistic creation, children, and gardening. But for thousands of years, the dwelling—the home— has sheltered all of these pursuits that make life worth living. The home is a place that gathers all kinds of activities, but that doesn't mean it has to be overly complex.

In his wonderful book *The Poetics of Space*, the philosopher Gaston Bachelard wrote, "The home is a place that shelters dreaming." He meant that the homes that nurture us are not fortresses of exclusion, but rather clearings in a busy world that help us to dream new ideas and to be creative in our own way. That's the greatest gift of the simple home. It's not the style or "design," but how we end up living and growing there that matters. A home is simply beautiful not so much for how it first appears, but for what the people who live there can become.

Chapter Two   Simple Is Enough

Indulge in the Luxury of Enough The ancient Greek philosopher Epicurus was a sage of modest pleasures and simple abundance. He believed that anxiety about status, wealth, and having more was the single greatest obstacle to human happiness. No matter how wealthy we are, we can't be happy if we crave more riches. No matter how much fame and pleasure come to us, we won't enjoy them if we hunger for greater thrills. Epicurus understood the good life as a simple life where the modest pleasures of home and hearth—good foods, gardens, and conversations—are the ultimate luxury. Contentment arises when we feel a gratitude for what we have, when we revel in the "luxury of enough."

The luxury of enough stems from knowing what you love and how you want to live at home. When you think about it, the modest pleasures of living—winter sunlight, the smell of coffee, the feel of moss—are surprisingly easy to bring into your home environment and daily routines. The journey is to find your own modest pleasures. The luxury of simplicity starts with understanding your own true tastes and throwing out notions of what you *should* have and like. You know you need somewhere to eat, but do you really need a separate dining room? You may really want the latest Viking® range, but how much cooking do you really do at home? Do you really need it?

Discovering the Simple Home within Us A simple home is not something you buy or assemble; it is something that you discover within yourself. The next time you are thinking about a home project, don't grab for the glossy design magazines and books (except this one, of course). Instead, you might slow down and begin a "place journal," a quiet written diary of the feelings, sounds, and movement in your envisioned den or porch or cabin. Write a narrative of what it would feel like to walk into that room after being away for several months. How would it feel on a dark winter night or on the first day of spring? What are the furnishings and activities in such a place? Make a list of adjectives. You can also think of a room that you loved as a child. Ask yourself the same questions and write about it. This is the process of discovering the simple home within you. It's not so much about what you want as *who you are*.

The study of yoga is another path to discovering the simple home inside. Part of the appeal of yoga is its focus on mindfulness directed at the most basic aspects of being alive, such as breathing and learning to invite stiff parts to move with the rest of the body. In building a home, such focus on movement translates into a simple domestic architecture that feels alive and evolves with you. So often excess tends to lose sight of essentials, and you end up with a kit of

parts or features. For any beloved home, the whole is greater than the sum of the parts. Like dancing or a child's song, there is a lack of analysis and pretension that is a luxury in itself.

Expressing Who We Really Are Simple luxuries are afforded as much by mindfulness as by big budgets. This chapter explores three outwardly different paths to the simplicity of enough. Yet, at their core, these three homes in upstate New York, San Francisco, and Minnesota share an authenticity in their expression of who their owners really are. These three houses express the careful choices of paring down.

Small is enough in each of these homes. Either built new or remodeled to fit today's lifestyles, they accommodate the way the owners really live. In upstate New York, simple abundance means a renovated farmhouse that preserves its original 18th-century rooms, comfortably heated and with old, wavy glass in new windows. It still has its authentic soul, a serene place where, because no mechanical noise is audible, the rustling of leaves is. In Minnesota, avoiding excess and keeping essentials in mind means skipping the dining room and affording the house, a new kind of farmhouse in a walkable new neighborhood at nature's edge.

The simplicity of enough becomes a luxury when it makes the most of where you live. In San Francisco, a tiny refrigerator makes sense because fresh food is available at the corner grocery. On the upstate New York farm, a whole mudroom is needed, because, to state the obvious, there's lots of mud. In Minnesota, the new farmhouse set in the prairie has lots of built-in storage by the doors for winter boots and summer baseball gear. In a four-season climate, it's simpler to build in such multipurpose storage units than to place a lot of space-consuming cabinets, shelves, dressers, and other specialized storage pieces around living and bedroom areas.

Each house in this section indulges in the simplicity of enough in a personal way for each owner. Yet shared among them all is the belief that having just enough of the right things is a privilege rather than a compromise. In a world of advertising messages that shout, "Buy this to express yourself!" having less translates into more. And, as Epicurus reminds us, unchecked acquisition can lead to tangible anxiety. So let's explore three house stories in the East, Midwest, and West, where people asked themselves Epicurean questions: What do I really want in my home and pursuits? How can I enjoy the simple abundance of daily life and create a home that's right for me?

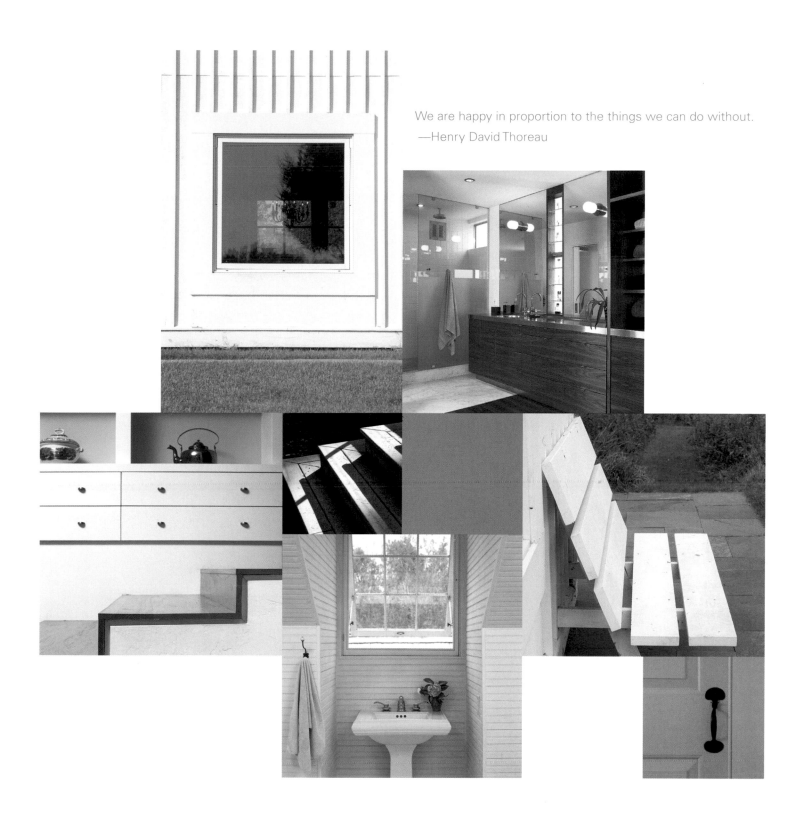

We are happy in proportion to the things we can do without.
—Henry David Thoreau

Down to the Bones

A Hudson Valley Farmhouse Lives Again

It's a dream of many to escape the bustle of the city and get away to a house in the country, where life can be lived at a simpler pace in bucolic surroundings. For Nicola, a British-born artist, the dream became a reality when she left her SoHo loft in New York City for an 18th-century Dutch Colonial farmhouse in the Hudson Valley. Newly renovated as a home and studio by architect Jim Joseph, the once "remuddled" house blooms again with restful wooden floors and plaster walls that catch the subtleties of light and shadow. This is a house of many textures, where nothing looks fake or feels manufactured.

Preserved from the original house, the cupboard stair with its tightly twisting steps calls to mind an earlier era of efficient simplicity. As a means to get upstairs, it is almost a piece of furniture, in marked contrast to the formal sweeping stair that would have been part of a grander colonial house.

A Place in History Simple houses can tell complex stories of their past. Such is the case with Nicola's farmhouse, which was built on 18th-century foundations and rebuilt many times. Although the area has a Dutch history dating back centuries, the house was probably constructed by a British dairy farmer with Puritan roots. Built frugally with lasting materials and well-proportioned small rooms, the tiny original house had been added onto twice during the 20th century (most recently with a makeshift addition in 1980). Rather than smoothing over all the level changes and quirky hallways, the redesign of the house emphasizes the fact that it has been built over time. Today, that layered growth with its somewhat random results feels authentic. For centuries, thrifty American farmers reused materials and often moved buildings to new locations. Nicola's farm tells such a story with reused timber from many eras and a kitchen addition that she believes was moved in from another site in the 1840s. Nothing remains of the original farmstead except some large pieces of timber incorporated into the red 19th-century barn.

Leaving the City Loft for the Country Farm As a palimpsest of many periods, the house has an awkwardness and spatial complexity that serves as a rich frame for the rehabilitation's straightforward finishes, windows, and wood floors. Nicola's friends thought she was crazy when she bought the place, but she fell in love with its haphazard quality the first time she visited the farm. Nicola is the first to say that her house has not been renovated for resale value. For many people, the small rooms and changes in floor levels seem contrary to a simple life in the country. Yet for Nicola, the house has an authentic soul that's the very essence of simplicity; for a painter, nothing could be more important for the simple, fruitful life.

→ Rebuilt with a new living room off the entry hall, the house has a quiet and still aesthetic born of editing out nonessential furnishings like overstuffed chairs and throw pillows. Reflected on the hall wall is light from the antique wavy glass used in the windows of the renovation.

Simple Solutions Hiding the New

The renovation intentionally emphasizes the fact that this house was built in bits and pieces over 150 years. With that in mind, modern improvements are, for the most part, kept out of sight. Heat is provided by radiant in-floor heating, which runs beneath the antique wood floors, and light switches are not in obvious places. In the front hall, an antique cupboard built into the wall hides the security system and other electronic devices.

In New York, Nicola's loft had big, empty spaces but nowhere to put anything. The high ceilings and light coming only from windows at the narrow end of the large, open room didn't feel intimate or cozy. In this house, Nicola likes the low ceilings in proportion to the intimate scale of the old rooms. The loft had only a perfunctory kitchen; this house has a real farmhouse kitchen with a serious stove. For a young artist, New York City was invigorating and edgy. Ten years later, the country beckoned as a calm foil.

A House Reborn Step inside the house, and it's as though you're stepping back in time. Sheltered under the gentle sweep of a simple entry porch, the front door opens onto an entryway that sets the tone for the rest of the house, with spare walls and trim, an unfinished floor, and minimal furnishings. To the left, what looks like the oldest part of the house is in fact the most recent addition: a quiet living room with a colonial green mantel, Puritan in its lack of a shelf. To the right of the entry hall, a step down leads into the hardest-working part of the house, with its large kitchen, brick-floored mudroom, and, beyond that, the studio.

In the kitchen, a cupboard stair climbs steeply to the second floor and its unlikely under-the-eave space. This compressed, low-ceilinged hallway opens into the gable-ceilinged bedroom, offering a great feeling of release as you come into the room. Retaining historic materials from the 1840s, the bedroom walls and ceiling are boards painted a crisp white. Tall, deep dormers flood the room with light and provide a nook for a desk.

Revealing the Spirit of the Old A simple analogy for the renovation of the house is Nicola's collection of found bones and branches from the property, which she arranges on bureaus and other surfaces throughout the house. Over the last century, the soul of Nicola's house has been buried by misguided alterations, leaving only the pieces of original structure, like the bones and

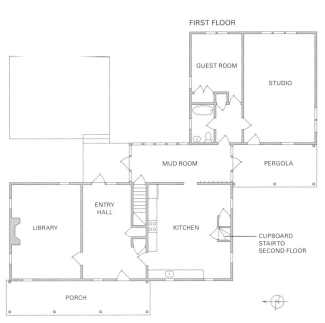

FIRST FLOOR

GUEST ROOM

STUDIO

MUD ROOM

PERGOLA

LIBRARY

ENTRY HALL

KITCHEN

CUPBOARD STAIR TO SECOND FLOOR

PORCH

← Devoid of ornament and Puritan in its simplicity, the living room is focused on the over-sized mantel. Double-hung windows custom-made with antique glass flank the mantel and give a view of the farmland outside. True to the historic character of the room, the lighting is colonial brought up to date with electricity.

↑ Kitchen cabinets, designed by architect Jim Joseph and inspired by mid-19th-century farmhouses, go with the built-in soapstone sink with its exposed front. Open shelves call to mind a simple farmhouse kitchen.

→ The drama of the deep bedroom dormer contrasts with the intimacy of the table Nicola likes to use for sketching.

← The mudroom, with its brick floor, is the heart and soul of an authentic farmhouse. The mudroom door, which leads directly to the vegetable garden, is one of six exterior doors.

↑ ↑ Retaining historic materials from the 1840s, the walls and ceilingboards are painted a crisp white A portrait by Nicola hangs over the bed.

↑ The tightly wound cupboard stair leads from the kitchen into this upstairs hall, which feels sheltered under the low gable ceiling. Straight ahead and up a few steps, the cathedral ceiling in the bedroom soars above the canopy bed.

branches that she collects. In seeking a simple home, Nicola saw a chance to start a new life cycle, to re-create the historic farm that might have been here. As evidence of life, death, and rebirth, Nicola saw the house not as a historic object but as an opportunity for the revelation of something new from the bones of the old. Starting with the bones meant keeping the foundations. As a result, every room is at a slightly different level—part of the soul that drew Nicola to the farm in the first place.

The Promise of House and Land To protect the land, the woman who sold the farm to Nicola placed a conservation easement on the land title that precludes the building of large housing developments. Over the last several years, Nicola has taken advantage of a federal grant to restore the land as native habitat for migratory birds and other species. As with the house itself, she is peeling back the layers of misguided human intervention to reveal the site's innate ecology and capacity for life. She bought a tractor to maintain the recently restored native grasses on the old farm fields.

Nicola's home is not a replica of the farm at any given point in time, and it's not fully "authentic" by strict historical standards because so much has been added. But in the spirit of the Hudson Valley and the English and Dutch settlers who farmed it, this place is very close to the land and the excellence that they achieved in craftsmanship and building. Like her paintings, it's a joyful and somewhat moody place that responds to daylight and the seasons. For Nicola, it's also true to her own creative quests at this phase of her life, and that may be the home's most authentic trait of all.

→ A farmhouse is the quintessential home, born out of practical necessity. Here, the small white house is dwarfed and protected from the road by the large L-shaped red barn.

Simple in Spirit "I fell in love with the place in its original condition. Dilapidated and humble though the buildings were, they had soul. I felt it immediately. I liked the feeling of awkwardness about the old house—for instance, no two floors were on the same level, and we kept that in the renovation, so there are steps up and steps down. It's not restful that way; it's a struggle and an adventure, like being on an illogical ship. From room to room, nothing is predictable."

—Nicola

Simple in the City

A Modern Townhouse for a Pared-Back Life

You don't have to live in a country cottage to lead a simple life. This 1,800-sq.-ft. San Francisco townhouse with a casual and open design shows an alternate path to paring back on life's complexity. A few years ago, Martin lived in a large Craftsman-style house of many rooms, each with a specialized purpose for entertaining, formal dining, sunning, eating breakfast, or reading a book. When the small house next door came on the market, he saw the opportunity to create a new kind of home with expansive views and a lot less clutter both inside and out.

Because Martin's new home is in the middle of a diverse and walkable city, it doesn't have to be a self-sufficient answer to all of life's needs. There are several markets for

The second floor of this San Francisco townhouse is an open, multipurpose space that combines kitchen, living, and dining areas. Overhead, a skylight admits light into the heart of the three-in-one room, illuminating the cooking/dining island that is set at an angle within the space.

fresh vegetables, fruit, and meat within easy walking distance. The payoff is that Martin doesn't need a freezer or even a large refrigerator. For him, this minimal home, while very convenient, is also a retreat from the buzz of work and city life. Its peacefulness makes the experience of simply going outside fun. Yet the landscape is also part of the experience of being inside. His home offers impressive views near and far. From inside the main level, he can look in one direction at the intimate Buena Vista Park and out the other side across Cole Valley and beyond to the Golden Gate Bridge and the Pacific Ocean.

Modern Fits In The one-bedroom home, with a separate guest suite tucked below in the hillside, replaces an undistinguished 1940s house that had been broken up into four bedrooms with almost no windows to enjoy the view. Architect Cass Calder Smith created a design that brings the cityscape inside while respecting the height and footprint of the original house within the narrow 20-ft.-wide lot. Today, the neighbors love this small gem with its quiet identity that doesn't compete with the Victorian and Craftsman houses on either side. Smith accomplished this feat with a façade that is both simple and rich without trying to copy the past. One large window on the front echoes the size of the bay window on the house next door, and the garage door is recessed so as not to dominate the house. A brown scrim of cedar slats creates a base for the floating band of windows above, providing privacy for the hall window at the lower level. Projecting out from the front façade above the driveway, a simple overhang helps to humanize the scale of the garage while giving a nod to San Francisco's grand old painted ladies with their ornate front porches.

↑ ← The extent of the view from the back deck was a pleasant surprise to the owner during the construction of his new home. The original house on the site had only tiny windows facing this view.

↑ In this compact-living home, basic kitchen needs (including a small refrigerator) are contained under the stainless-steel counter of the island. At the far end, an attached walnut table provides dining space for six.

← Wedged between a turn-of-the-century Victorian and an elaborate 1920s Craftsman, this low modern house blends seamlessly into the neighborhood with a simple façade and restrained color palette.

Three Rooms in One In a reversal of most house plans, the public spaces are housed upstairs in one airy, all-purpose room, and the bedroom and bathroom (just one) are downstairs. Martin claims to have a 900-sq.-ft. living room, a 900-sq.-ft. kitchen, and a 900-sq.-ft dining room. They all just happen to be the same room. With no interior walls and almost all the furniture built in, this multipurpose room feels surprisingly spacious. The restrained color palette of walnut floors, white walls, and stainless steel enhances the effect.

Natural daylight washes the center of the large island from a skylight and a tall, narrow window. At the head of the stairs, a glass panel in the floor drops light into the hall that leads to the bedroom. Each end of the main room is a window wall that wraps a corner in a classic modernist reference. Such strategies address the age-old problem in townhouses where light comes from only the narrow front and back, and the side walls are necessarily windowless.

Living with Less Like a refined short essay, this house is rich in nuances and careful transitions because it cannot afford to waste words. The subtle angle of the built-in couch in the living room and the inviting spaces throughout challenge traditional symmetries and bring a surprising richness to this serene city home. While the house is an icon of the dot-com era, Martin's orderly and stripped-down life has much older roots in the California school of modernism of Richard Neutra and Charles Eames, who made the most of contemporary industrial materials, broad windows, and expansive views.

→ Downstairs, the bathroom and bedroom flow together as a single room (the wardrobe shelves tie into the base cabinet of the vanity). In the bedroom, light enters from a small window high in the storage wall to balance light from the large windows. Out in the open and meticulously organized, clothing is part of the look of the room.

→ ↑ Consistent with the clean lines of the rest of the house, a built-in storage platform in the bedroom is made of the same walnut used for the floors and other built-in items. Devoid of trim, the only decoration is provided by the small stainless-steel recessed pulls.

FIRST FLOOR

DECK   BEDROOM   BATH   ENTRY   GARAGE

SECOND FLOOR

SKYLIGHT ABOVE   LIVING ROOM   FIRE "ORB"   KITCHEN   DINING

To fit all of life's necessities into this compact house, Martin closely examined his daily needs and came to the conclusion that he could do without an oven and other kitchen items that most would consider essential. But there were some things he couldn't do without. A marvel of smart house technology, the kitchen has a computer monitor sitting on the central island and a hard drive hidden below that controls the heating system, lighting, audiovisual components, and LCD projector. For watching movies, the LCD projector shines on a white wall in the seating area. In lieu of a large flat-screen TV, it can just be turned off, and no complex cabinetry or mounting is required. Living with less extends to the television.

Pockets of Warmth Martin's house feels bigger and more inviting because it is filled with pockets of quiet warmth, such as the roof garden and the cantilevered kitchen table that extends the cooking island for small gatherings. One of the more unusual retreats is the suspended spherical "fire orb," a metallic fireplace that seems to float over the city view. Having no oven doesn't preclude the social ritual of a cookout. For a recent dinner party, Martin served a menu of fresh sardines grilled in the fireplace.

Martin's house challenges our assumptions that modern homes are rigid and cold. His house is a garden of calm in a busy city, a modern design that fits into a historic neighborhood. He made the choice to pare back on space and possessions to create a home where the delights of simplified living and entertaining in the middle of a rich and complex city are more than enough.

→ Corner windows in the living area open up a far-reaching view toward the Pacific Ocean, while the futuristic stainless-steel "fire orb" floating above a round of white marble provides a cozy focus for the built-in seating area.

Island in a Box Striking out at an angle across the open upstairs living and kitchen area, the 30-ft. island is a bold design move within the strictlyrectangular room. Combining walnut at the dining-table end and stainless steel at the kitchen end, the island is a stand-alone work of art that's also highly functional. On the island side away from the stairs, the under-counter refrigerator and storage units make up a simple kitchen. On the stair side, stools tuck under the counter overhang, providing easy seating for using the computer to control the house systems and answer e-mail. At the far end, the island becomes a cantilevered table with dining space for six.

Little White House on the Prairie

A Home for Community and Play

For some people, moving an hour east of the city, where they work, to live in a meadow on a river bluff would seem like anything but a path to a simpler life. But for Shane and Kat, a landscape architect and photographer, respectively, the commute to the beautiful St. Croix River Valley and their new neighborhood, Jackson Meadow, is the best choice they ever made. With a young son and daughter, the couple wanted a place where the kids could explore the woods, where neighbors' children could run through the yard, and where you could hear the slam of a screen door.

When do you know you have enough? Enough possessions? Enough indoor and outdoor space? Homeowners are often convinced that they need rooms and features like hot

The simple gable form evokes both the farmhouses on Minnesota's prairie and the fishermen's houses of Lake Superior, near where the architect grew up. Dramatically oversized trim makes the house feel even smaller than its compact size.

tubs and fireplaces that turn out to be unnecessary. They also think that "nature" can be experienced only by moving to large-lot developments with broad sweeps of lawns. In moving to Jackson Meadow, a housing development where Shane is landscape architect and architect David Salmela is the designer, the couple sought that increasingly rare blend of a kid-scaled neighborhood at the edge of nature: a walkable village connected to safe and beautiful landscapes for the unsupervised play they remembered from their own childhoods.

Trade-Offs for Simplicity Shane and Kat's tall, thin meadow house is a story of trade-offs, of building within the budget the bank would allow. At the start of the planning process, it was clear that their budget would not stretch to cover everything that most new homes contain. So Shane and Kat eliminated rooms typically considered basic, such as a dining room and a master bath. Instead, the family considers it a bonus to brush their teeth together in the one upstairs bathroom. The table in the kitchen serves for dinner, cooking projects, and afternoon coffee with neighbors. And the woodstove that they'd contemplated was a $5,000 option cut from the budget. Four years later, they hardly miss it.

At the most basic level of design thrift, the narrow floor plan requires only standard-dimension lumber to span the width of the house. The interior is brightened with the choice of low-cost yellow birch for wood flooring, trim, and cabinets. Upstairs, the floors are the lowest grade of oak, painted and sealed to add color.

Learning from the Past As with many other simple homes, this house grows out of the time-tested economies of vernacular building traditions. The houses at Jackson Meadow are inspired by their location in the village of Marine on St. Croix, the oldest settlement in Minnesota, with small, white gabled houses that recall the New England roots of the early inhabitants.

↑ ← Floating away from the band of square windows, the stairway that leads out of the kitchen is a classic modern design. To the right of the stair wall, a multi-purpose built-in serves as buffet, file cabinet, and general catch-all storage space.

↑ With room for all that's needed—a comfy bed, a reading chair, and a television (along with a wall of built-in storage just out of view)—the master bedroom is the epitome of the "luxury of enough." The painted wood floor, made of seconds to save money, relieves the overall whiteness of the space.

← Simple is not always Shaker-spare. In this combination kitchen/dining room, the children's ceramic artwork shares shelf space with family photos, while an antique chandelier livens up the palette of white walls and blond cabinets. The small, dark building outside the kitchen window is the neighborhood water tower.

With its steep gables and simple windows, Shane and Kat's new home resonates with familiar traditional forms. Yet this house is much more than a quaint copy of the past. On the outside, Salmela's use of textures and trim widths reinvents ordinary elements in intriguing changes of scale, with small, square windows punched through broad façades and a wide stair leading to an intimate garage loft.

Inside, the open floor plan is simply ordered in a casual way with its main rooms—kitchen and living room—at either end of the house. Salmela calls these rooms the "go-to rooms," bookends that are bridged by the open central gathering space. This is a modern multipurpose floor plan that works for this family. The center space seems open and empty, a luxury of space in a small home. Yet it also serves as hall and a workspace, with two desks built into the striking 40-ft.-long counter that spans the full length of the house from front to back door.

Private Places and Family Fun In any family, especially one with a relatively small and open house, it's important to have a place where you can get away for some peace and quiet. One of the simplest, most traditional ways to do this is to build out the loft over the garage as a place where a parent can work alone or the kids can play with their friends. Walking there involves a trip outside, and an opportunity for fresh air that would be missed by walking down a hall. Using the space above the garage for this added room was less expensive than adding more space to the main house— another ingenious choice.

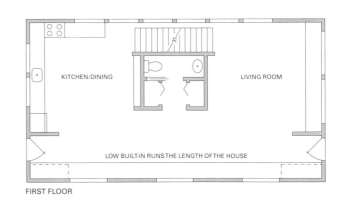

KITCHEN/DINING   LIVING ROOM

LOW BUILT-IN RUNS THE LENGTH OF THE HOUSE

FIRST FLOOR

→ Living large in a small house is possible with a multipurpose space that includes two built-in desks with a view for homework. Part hallway and part room, this transitional space connects the living room and the kitchen (and serves as a holiday dining room with a long table set up for Thanksgiving).

→ → The second-floor hallway connects the three bedrooms and leads to the only bathroom upstairs. Midway along the hall, a laundry chute dumps dirty clothes into the utility room below, a simple, everyday efficiency.

↑ The space above the garage provides an "away room" a short distance from the small main house, perfect for working, reading, spreading out a project, or simple contemplation. The floorboards are seconds, painted a sandy yellow to anchor the spare furnishings.

↑ ↑ Simple solves practical problems in an elegant way. Doors to the left and right conceal laundry machines and the heating system and also create an anteroom to the downstairs bath (which features one of Kat's paintings). Flanking the anteroom are small wall-inset shrines, one for each child of the house to do with as they please.

← Lining up with the view down the valley, the square window anchors one end of the living room and also forms part of the storage/desk/bench that runs the length of the house. Two photographs by Kat frame the window, and simple light fixtures complete the picture.

The owners' taste is a blend of modern and antique sensibilities that fill this simple white home with color. Antique chandeliers, the two kids' clay creations, a Persian coffee table, and Kat's photography all bring a sense of humanity and a fun feeling to the interior. This is a house that does not take itself too seriously. Each child chose their own favorite color for the window trim in their bedroom, providing a joyful contrast to the limited palette in the rest of the house.

Neighborly Connections Setting the house in its landscape as a white ornament, Salmela planned the home and garage/studio to connect to the site with repeated windows framing views out of all sides of the house. Because of the narrow floor plan, you're aware of both side views—the long one down the valley and the intimate one to the woods to the south. Shane often spends time alone or with neighbors at a fire pit behind the house near the woods. Kids and adults sit on big fieldstones and trade stories around the fire at twilight. There is a kind of simplicity in community life that has no price, and it need not require elaborate community parks and gardens.

Many people think of white modernism as stark and uncomfortable. This meadow house conveys a stripped-down elegance that includes comfort and a sense of humor. Small and seemingly plain from a distance, the house is subtly inventive, with a richness of texture and details that comes into focus as you draw near. The narrow floor plan, the repeated large and small square window patterns, the straight view from front to back doors all leave you with a sense that this linear house is not really small, but rather shiplike, floating on its inland sea of grass, moored at the shoreline of woods and meadow, where the prairie begins.

Simple in Community Jackson Meadow is a 145-acre development on a bluff-top clearing of restored prairie outside the Twin Cities. With the exception of the water-tower structure, all 64 houses are painted white, standing out among the prairie grasses. On winter nights, they blend into the snowfields with the gentle blue cast of moonlight. There is a strong sense of community here, where neighbors walk on the roads and kids make paths in the woods. The design of the houses, their sites, and the neighborhood as a whole work together to create a sense of visual, architectural, and social connection, much like an old city neighborhood or small town.

Some simple strategies for weaving homes into a community are to build the houses close together while preserving the surrounding open space and views. Jackson Meadow's homes cluster on less than a third of the available site, leaving a large common nature preserve. All the streets are the width of typical 19th-century village streets to reduce speed and create a more pedestrian scale for neighborly visits, and there are no streetlights, so you can see the stars at night, a rare treat in our electrified world.

Village scale is made real here by allowing outbuildings, like Shane and Kat's studio/garage, and restricting house plans to 24 ft. wide with 12-in-12 pitched metal roofs. All the houses are white, and floor plans are rectangular and simple in form, with the functional unity of a New England village.

Chapter Three Simple Is Flexible

A Comfortable, Multipurpose Home *Comfort* and *luxury* don't have to mean lots of rooms, each with a limited purpose. With thoughtful insight into what you value and how you spend your time, you can create a home where life's events flow together. Who needs a Victorian mansion with separate rooms for sewing, arranging flowers, entertaining the minister, and playing the piano? In thinking that we need a house of many rooms, we forget the many hours and years that we have to work to pay for them. The simple home offers the luxury of actually being able to spend time at home with people and pursuits that you enjoy.

Instead of paying for, vacuuming, and walking though lots of rooms, consider creating rooms with overlapping purposes, such as a quiet den that doubles as a guest room, a storage pantry that also makes a great place to wrap presents and packages for shipping. Life is simpler when rooms are well planned for multiple purposes, easy to maintain, and comfortable. The popularity of the declutter movement is a testament to the benefits of sorting and selecting rather than building ever-bigger houses.

Comfort Comes in Many Styles The houses in this chapter show how it is possible to create flowing and open rooms without the potential starkness of an artist's loft or the minimalism of a modern art gallery, where one dropped tissue can ruin the whole effect. Such extreme modernism or conspicuous minimalism leaves a bad taste for many who seek comfort. Houses in this section include a new suburban home with a traditional look, a new home incorporating traditional elements with its old barn parts and pieces, and a midcentury remodel that brings a sunny dining/living room to a once-partitioned rambler.

Achieving multipurpose simplicity in your rooms, workspaces, and furniture (both built-in and freestanding) requires some thought. In this section, we include houses that exude the freedom and comfort of flexible design. They offer solutions for how to store things, ride an exercise bike, have a place for children to play, and make dinner—all in one room.

Uniting Work, Dining, and Play Although relatively small, the multifunctional homes shown here focus on spacious rooms that bring living, dining, and play together. Rooms can change purpose, like the breakfast area in the Minnesota house that also serves as a child's play area. In the Connecticut barn, the away room is up a flight of stairs. Here, *flexible* means an open home that embodies all the charm of a rambling old barn but is scaled down to a cozy domestic scale with a compact kitchen, sitting area, and eating area that flow together. Daylight streams down through the loft and glass floor to add to the delight of this space.

All entertaining and public purposes are brought together.

In California, where casual living was invented, comfort dictated that a remodel add modern, light-filled rooms for sitting and dining, all with an ocean view. *Comfortable* and *cozy* are closely related in our dreams about home. *Cozy* might describe a small stone cottage in Ireland with a fire burning in the large fireplace. In reality, this cottage had and likely still has cold stone floors, a low ceiling, and a few hard chairs to draw up to the smoky peat fire. But against the chilly damp outside, it is indeed cozy.

Do we own objects or do they possess us? Do we really need the large room of formal furniture (sometimes still covered in plastic wraps) waiting for visitors who rarely come? Despite the march of time and technology, *comfortable* still comes down to a favorite chair in a favorite place; simple comfort comes down to rooms that have many purposes—kitchens, window seats, and dens that become islands of calm in a fast-paced world.

The aspects of things that are most important for us are hidden because of their simplicity and familiarity.
—Ludwig Wittgenstein

The Stucco Gabled House

A Simple Home Grows with a Family

For Susan, a formative experience on her path to simplicity was a trip to Africa, where she met people who "lived with so little compared to us." Seeing villages and families whose wealth lay in community and in one another changed Susan's own sense of security and contentment. Her house, in an established postwar neighborhood just west of Minneapolis, reflects this yearning to scale back on clutter and the maintenance of the huge amount of "stuff" that characterizes American life. It's a house that focuses on people, on being together, and on openness and gathering places rather than on accessories to fill them up.

Nestled into a hilly postwar neighborhood just west of Minneapolis, this stucco-gabled house is a showcase of simple cost-saving building strategies for a home that grows with a family.

Susan bought the lot for the house when she was still single, with no idea about the kind of family she might someday have. There was already a house on the long, narrow lot, but as often happens renovating the house proved to be at least as expensive as building new. So Susan worked with architect Paul Buum to design an entirely new but traditional-looking home that could be phased for growth with thoughts of a future family (and budget) in mind. Now, a few years later, Susan is married with a young daughter, and her house has changed with her life, growing into the unfinished spaces as her family has grown.

One Great Room for Everyone Although the stucco and gabled façade could easily pass for an authentic Craftsman house, the interior is anything but traditional. The garage and service space, including mudroom, pantry, half-bath, stair, and office, are all placed to the front of the house, allowing the living spaces to be set to the back, overlooking a creek at the end of the 250-ft.-long lot. Rather than a center hall and separate dining, kitchen, and living areas, a front porch provides entry to a short hall that steps right into the lofty great room, with open areas for living, dining, and cooking, as well as a breakfast nook.

For Susan, a simpler life means finding more time to spend with others. Remembering her trip to Africa, when she began to plan the house with Buum she knew that she wanted a large and simple open space where everyone would feel welcome at a gathering rather than isolated in separate rooms. In many ways, this public area has the feel of a large urban loft, one great room that works for everyone, all the time.

→ Tucked up under a gable at the back of the house, the master bedroom, with its inviting window seat and restful yellow and white color palette, overlooks the creek below. The built-in not only provides a cozy place to sit but also a thrifty way to conceal the heating duct for the room.

FIRST FLOOR

Making Small Spaces Bigger Simple houses tend to be small, but they don't have to feel confining. A good strategy for opening up a great room is to create a sense of public scale and connection to the outside. Paul Buum designed the great room's ceiling height to create what designers call "spatial compression and release." It's an old trick used by Frank Lloyd Wright and other residential designers to draw visitors into a house with a relatively low hall and vestibule ceilings. The visitor then steps down a foot or two into the living area with its outward views and slightly taller floor-to-ceiling height. The effect is rather like stepping from a cave into the outdoors, and it is a simple tactic to make a small house grand and surprising.

Though the communal room is only 24 ft. wide, it feels much larger. The living room is set off from kitchen and dining areas with a 2-ft. bump-out toward the creek and a tongue-and-groove wood ceiling that stands apart from the painted plaster ceilings of the rest of the room. Structural posts help to anchor the living room. The openness of the room not only saves on the costs of interior walls but also allows all areas to enjoy light from three sides. The effect is that both the wooden floor and ceiling planes add charm and distinct character to each of the four living areas while unifying them as a great public space filled with daylight.

Overlooking the creekside woods and garden in back, Susan's great room brings everyone together for holiday meals and casual lunches. And the open space embraces changing uses as the family changes. Currently, the breakfast nook next to the kitchen is occupied by a child-scale play kitchen used by Susan's daughter. When Susan cooks, her daughter bakes and mixes right alongside her, learning from watching her mom, but most important, just being with her.

Building in Phases Finishing off every room in a house all at once can be an expensive proposition. The fact that Susan had to phase construction as she could afford it actually added to the house's flexibility as her family grew in unpredictable ways. Upstairs, phases two and three built out the child's bedroom along with a third bedroom over the garage that has worked

↑ The multipurpose space between the kitchen island and the back deck is currently used as a play area with its own tiny kitchen. Once the daughter grows out of this space, it will become a breakfast nook for the whole family.

↓ In keeping with the simple palette throughout the house, the mirror surround and vanity in the bathroom are fir, which matches the beams in the downstairs ceiling. Essentials are stowed in the vanity drawers, with room for treasures on the shelf that floats below.

→ Simple in its white-on-white composition of tile and drywall, the fireplace surround is a quiet focus for the seating area. Overhead, the decking and beamed ceiling define this area as separate from the rest of the great room.

both as a home office and a domain for a visiting teenager. Phase three also saw the completion of the master bathroom.

Building in phases was not the only strategy for containing costs. With budget in mind, architect Buum chose ordinary 2-in. by 2-in. posts for the handrails and relatively inexpensive two-over-one windows that evoke a Craftsman feel while framing large, uninterrupted views. Behind the scenes, using standard-size materials such as precut studs and eliminating all unnecessary walls were additional cost-saving strategies.

Right for the Site The simplicity of scale and spatial arrangement evident in the house also works at the level of the overall home site. The house is set back from the street to save existing trees (including a gnarled old cedar right next to the garage), which has the added benefit of making it seem as though the house has always been there. The massive garage presence of many suburban houses is further softened with two single garage doors, 7 ft. high and 8 ft. wide, a bit tight for gargantuan SUVs but better scaled to house and street. And instead of a manicured front lawn, the area next to the driveway is a free-form garden planted with flowers and prairie grasses.

From the start, this house has met Susan's needs. As budget allowed, she has improved interior finishes and materials such as the kitchen island, originally a low-cost plastic laminate that she recently upgraded to black granite. Currently, she is working with Buum to complete phase four, the enclosure of a screened porch under the living-room balcony. In theory, this is the last of the phased projects, but with a simple house this flexible and open to change, new ideas and possibilities are endless.

→ Connected to the great room via the overhead beams and columns, the kitchen is part of yet separate from the rest of the room. Upper cabinets are confined to an interior wall, opening up the kitchen to views through the large double-hung windows. The granite countertop on the island is an upgrade from the thrifty plastic laminate original.

Domesticate the Garage Many of today's suburban houses are overwhelmed by massive three-car garages that create an opaque and uninviting street façade. Susan knew she didn't want to go that route. Architect Paul Buum came up with some simple strategies to make a two-car garage feel right at home in a neighborhood of small houses. Side-by-side doors instead of one large door reduce the scale of the garage, as does the lower height of the garage gable, and the window box above adds a domesticated touch. Stained a similar color to the indoor fir trim, the doors are accented with small, off-center windows that bring the fine-grain patterns of the living areas outside. Set back to the left, the inviting front porch with its detail of railings and porch furniture draws family and visitors away from the driveway.

A Simple Barn

A Small Design Lives Large

It's hard to think of a simpler form than the classic New England barn. Built for function and value, the practical barn makes the most of the available space within a simple gable roof and rectangular form. Openings are designed for moving feed and animals in and out, and the design expresses daily farm routines with a simple beauty.

Such classic simplicity can inspire comfortable, multipurpose new houses today. Barbara Garfield, the original client and codesigner for this small, sophisticated house, knows how to make a home that is cozy, efficient, expansive, and yet small. A collaboration with designer David Howard, this barn-inspired home draws on Barbara's

Built with reclaimed barn beams, the open, multipurpose main room of this compact house combines cooking, eating, and relaxing. A walkway bridge overhead provides a subtle separation between the kitchen and living room (at left), while a beam from the bridge to the outside wall defines the dining area from the kitchen.

childhood memories of farm visits to relatives, a compact interpretation of a Yankee barn as the stage for life's daily activities rather than a stage set for display. The result is a remarkably functional and flexible design of 1,200 sq. ft. divided among three floors.

Graceful Living on a Small Footprint The three-level, multipurpose design succeeds in reducing square footage rather than function. The house has a footprint of only 870 sq. ft., a scale that makes daylight all the more important in connecting inside and outside and reducing the claustrophobic effects of interior rooms. To stream light through all three levels, Howard came up with a three-dimensional skylight at the peak of the roof and a glass floor for the upper loft (where visitors or grandkids sleep). As a mark of his success, visitors to the house invariably comment on the wonderful play of light as well as the cozy feel engendered by the well-proportioned rooms and large windows.

Facing southeast, the two-story main room connects cooking, eating, relaxing, and doing homework in one open space. Yet, balancing this openness, the home also offers cozy nooks for retreat, such as the master bedroom secluded by an inset hallway off the dining room and the office/music loft tucked in a quiet corner on the second floor (what Howard calls an "I-want-to-be-by-myself room"). Living here, you can be part of the main event or off quietly reading a book. What this house doesn't have are fancy rooms for public display, the sort of parlors that stand unused unless the preacher comes calling.

→ In a tiny house, the delight of this two-story glass space is particularly unexpected. The glass railings along the walkway above allow light to filter down from the rooftop skylight.

→ → The large skylight at the top of the house lets light fall on either side of the walkway bridge down to the first floor. The bridge itself leads to the loft office/music room, with a "sleeping box" behind the half wall to the left for a child or an overnight guest. Candles along the railing wait for night to add drama to the dining area below.

FIRST FLOOR

SECOND FLOOR

Floor plan labels, First Floor: LIVING ROOM, MASTER BEDROOM, KITCHEN, DINING ROOM, ENTRY

Floor plan labels, Second Floor: MUSIC ROOM/OFFICE/DEN, OPEN TO BELOW, BEDROOM, LADDER TO THIRD STORY, LOFT, BRIDGE, SLEEPING BOX, OPEN TO BELOW

Connected to Where You Are Historically, functional yot oom fortable vernacular houses and farm buildings made sensible use of stone, wood, and other materials available locally. Today, whether renovating or building new, part of being connected to where you are comes from making the indigenous materials of the land visible in the building. Connecticut is nothing if not rocky, which is why so many pioneers ultimately moved west to find better farmland. The stone foundations and walls of the region live on today in farms and overgrown woods.

This is a home that feels authentic because, along with the stone foundation, its post-and-beam structure of salvaged chestnut beams carries the patina of old growth, age, and reuse. With its soaring two-story windows bringing southeast light into the dining and kitchen areas, and its solid grid of beams and skylight perched at rooftop, this shingled house is a study in solidity and airiness.

The idea of reusing an old barn with its hand-hewn timbers is a frequent dream, but not often a practical reality. Instead, this new home was designed to resemble a barn with a steep gable and a large hayloft opening at one end. Barbara found the historic old beams in a classified ad in the local paper one lucky morning, and because her home is a completely new building, its scale could be miniaturized. The result is a human-scaled tribute to a large barn that, in reality, would have been sized for a drive-in hay wagon and hay for a long winter.

↑ Tall corner windows create a sunny spot for a favorite reading chair set on the stone floor of the master bedroom. For privacy, the windows in this room only have interior shutters, which are in keeping with the barn aesthetic.

↓ The large window into the living room is a scaled-down version of the large opening in the gable end of a barn that would admit the business of farming. The barn-door shutters with their sliding hardware have a whimsical square-cut opening for a long-forgotten purpose.

→ In the white kitchen at the heart of the house, traditional stile-and-rail cabinet doors contrast with nontraditional concrete counters. Wide-board floors complement the rough post-and-beam structure.

New and Old Work Together Part of multifunctional design is seeking out the best materials and solutions from many eras to make a home that is relevant for life today. We look backward with longing at simpler times and the comforting familiarity of colonial farms, yet we also want to have home entertainment systems for music and film. Even though this small barn is a new design with modern appliances, its shingle siding and roof pitch evoke images of the iconic New England farm building.

On the outside, a traditional language of shingle siding and many-paned windows stacked in geometric patterns contrasts with the wildness of the surrounding woods. The small windows provide an intimacy to rooms where appropriate, such as bathrooms and bedrooms. Inside, rooms lit by these traditional windows are white, open, and freely connected. The modern, white interior is concealed in a rustic traditional shell, creating a wonderful balance of new and old, rough and smooth. Yet, true to Barbara's style, all the barn's surfaces and materials are simple and basic.

Today, the barn is home to Diane and Bill, who settled here after several years in Switzerland. For this couple, moving to Connecticut is a return to a simpler life, where a quart of milk is the destination of a morning's walk and the pace of life includes stopping to say hello to neighbors. When asked how she is simplifying her daily life, Diane points out that they are scaling back from eight sofas to one! As a small, multipurpose house, this Connecticut barn, like the beams that give it structure, will continue to be passed down through the generations. In its timeless simplicity, it will accommodate new owners and lifestyles, and even as fashions come and go, the comforting logic of its simple materials, spaces, and roof shape will live on.

← The bookcase wall surrounding the fireplace is the focal point of the living room. Although the white grid of the bookcase is modern in feel, its top molding ties it in with the traditional surroundings. Overhead, the underside of the loft floor is built of reclaimed barn timber left natural with white-stained decking in between for a simple, clean look.

↑ The modest detailing of the front entry—with simple plank door, full-width divided light transom, and hand-wrought hardware—borrows from nearby colonial houses. The no-nonsense light adds an authentic barnyard touch.

Simple Addition

Opening Up for Entertaining

Is it simpler to tear down an existing house or to add on? For Ida and Bill, keeping their postwar bungalow on its ocean-front site made sense in a neighborhood of tear-downs. They loved the one-level home's 1950s feel with its streamlined horizontal windows and plain white façades. However, in the existing house, entertaining was always a challenge. As in many small beach houses of the time, one room served as the living room, dining room, and public space. For a dinner party, the dining table had to be pulled out from the wall and the living-room furniture pushed out of the way. Hardly the best arrangement.

The addition to this 1950s California bungalow provides a much better connection between the house and garden than in the original design, with spaces for entertaining both inside and out, all with a view of the ocean beyond.

In addition, the original house sat high above the backyard, not unlike a trailer up on blocks. The initial plan was simply to add a dining room and find a way to connect the living spaces with the garden on the ocean side. But architect Taal Safdie, of Safdie Rabines Architects, had a better idea, suggesting the addition of a cascade of spaces on the back side to connect the house and garden. The long, loftlike addition not only adds more flexible living and dining space, but also brings people through the house to the almost-forgotten outdoor space. The back side of the house now opens at three levels onto new decks that step down to the garden, with the tallest space in the new living room. By creating such improved indoor-outdoor connections, the addition has the flexibility to open up to the new decks and the yard for large gatherings.

The proof is in the parties. For their silver wedding anniversary, Ida and Bill transformed the house into a kind of outdoor pavilion, throwing open all the doors, moving the living-room couches out onto the deck, and serving cocktails in the garden. Dinner for 22 was served on tables set up in the living room and in the dining room, with after-dinner dancing on the outdoor stone terrace steps down from the deck. And all this was made possible by adding just one room.

↑ The long, loftlike addition completely transforms the look of the original cramped, dark house, not only adding more flexible living and dining space, but also bringing new life to the existing home.
→ → Connecting the old and new house and running the full length of the house, the storage display wall unifies the various living spaces in the one-room addition. Defined within the larger open area to give a sense of separation, the living area has a tile floor and is four steps down from the dining floor level. In addition, pillars separate the space from the flow of the atrium.

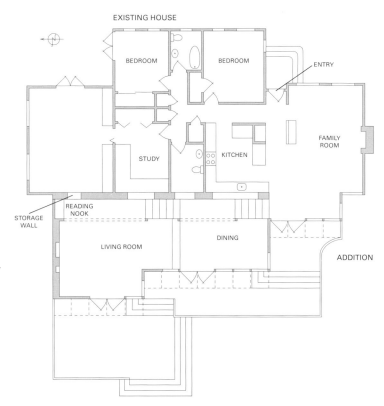

Light and Life for Spaces Old and New Arriving at the non
descript bungalow on the street side, you'd never suspect that
the house has been transformed with a new addition. The front
door, which originally entered a cramped vestibule, now opens
directly to the former living room with a clear visual connection
to the kitchen and the ocean-view addition. An addition can all
too often leave the existing rooms without purpose as leftover
spaces or pass-through rooms, but that's not the case here.
Both the former living room, now a multipurpose family room,
and the kitchen have new life as a hub for family activities (or a
quiet time by the fireplace).

But the main event is the long one-room addition along the
back wall of the house, connected by an atrium with a wall of
built-in storage. Matching the ceiling height in the existing
house, the levels of the addition cascade down to the garden
level. On the first landing, the new dining area has a built-in buffet, which also forms a low wall to the living room. As the floor
levels step down, the ceiling heights in the different parts of the
addition step up. The living-room ceiling is dramatically higher,
which invites guests to descend and enjoy the larger open
space, culminating in a cozy reading nook at the far end.

When you add on, the danger is that the rooms in the original house may be cut off from views that they formerly enjoyed.
But Safdie came up with a simple solution that not only preserves the views but actually improves them. By incorporating

→ The steps cascade down the addition, terminating in a cozy reading nook at the
end of the atrium. At the top of the stairs, the dining room is close to the kitchen
and visually connected to the living room below. High clerestory windows flood
the space with light.
→ → With their deep treads and shallower-than-standard rise, the steps reinforce
the horizontal feel of the house—and the sense of flowing down the site. Careful
detailing with clean lines, just a slim line of wood trim, and restrained hardware
create a simple, elegant feel.

A Flexible Storage Wall The exterior wall between an existing house and a new addition is a space that is often overlooked when adding on, but here it is reborn as a functional storage space that runs the full length of the house. The wall is the depth of the lower cabinets and provides storage for books, games, and electronics as well as display spaces for treasured objects. But the wall also serves as a seam between old and new, incorporating openings to rooms in the existing house, with shutters for privacy. Simple in its overarching design vision, the wall creates a unifying aesthetic for the rooms it connects.

openings into the storage wall where windows used to be, the addition offers connecting internal views from the study and kitchen into the new wing and beyond to the ocean. As an additional way to bring light into the existing rooms, the new wing is topped with clerestory windows over the stair that spill light into all parts of the house. As a beacon of light, the clerestory atrium becomes a seam that ties new and old together.

Connecting to the Garden The original house was almost a full flight of steps above the garden, which meant that it was separate and inaccessible from the house. Addressing this opportunity, the cascading addition opens out at three levels onto new decks that step down to the garden. Off the family room and one step down is the first deck, which invites you outside from the old house. Respecting the fall of the land and the existing native pines, the deck steps down and around the large tree at the back of the house.

At the back of the yard, a new gravel terrace is a quiet terminus, just the right ending for this updated beach house that connects inside and outside, midcentury and new. In a world of ever-bigger houses, we often assume that more space means more complication. In this house, just the right amount of space, well designed and flexible, helps to bring new life to an existing home while simplifying the daily lives—and certainly the parties—of the people who live there.

→ Tucked into the corner of the family room addition, a landing nook overlooking the deck provides a quiet spot for a read.
→ → Respecting the fall of the land and the existing native Torrey pines, the new deck steps down and around the large tree at the back of the house. To the right of the tree, the family room in the old part of the house is just visible, with a window pattern that is referenced in the addition.

Chapter Four Simple Is Thrifty

The Prosperity of Needing Less Simple thrift is about more than saving money. Rather, it's part of the prosperity of planning and making wise decisions. In designing the simple home, thrift can be a pathway to long-term bounty. Quite appropriately, the word *thrift*, as derived from Old Norse, is historically tied to the word *thrive*. By 14th-century Middle English, *thrift* meant the "condition of thriving and prosperity," a far stretch from its austere and budget-driven connotations today.

In this section, we visit four houses—in the city, in the desert, and on the water—that tell stories of their owners' forethought in identifying their most basic needs and values, the simple home within each of them. Like the maintenance of a savings account or an orchard, thrift is something that takes advance planning and persistence for its fruits to be born. In building a home, simple thriftiness takes place over time. It means spending less to build and maintain a home over the years. A home with relatively lower costs frees up time and money for the other bank accounts of life: time to spend with the kids, money to invest in their future education.

It's All about Value Thriftiness by design creates a prosperity of needing less. Yet, thrifty design doesn't necessarily mean small or unadorned. Rather, thrifty domestic architecture is really about value. In designing a home, thriftiness can be achieved by employing simple forms, an efficient floor plan, a smaller size, and recycled materials. The houses in this section are relatively inexpensive while offering the stability of long-term comfort and affordable upkeep. Whether the owner's primary goal was a healthy home and indoor air quality or a fun house with an elf door for a child, these houses focus on clear goals with playful and sometimes surprising results.

The simple and low-cost pleasures of fresh air and fresh food seem almost exotic in our convenient, plastic-wrapped world. One of the houses to follow is like a farmstead in the city with its own organic vegetable garden large enough to provide most of its owners' produce needs. In northwest Washington, the community activity of cooking and eating takes place around a large plank table in the Red Beach House, celebrating the most basic pleasures of tastes, smells, and being together.

In the high desert of New Mexico, thrift is expressed in a house that takes economy to fun places with its use of recycled parts and pieces. In Brooklyn, thrift is seen in a house that repeats a square theme in plan and section to create an efficient and comfortable home.

In the end, the simple thrifty home is about value, now and in the long term. It means knowing yourself and your own priorities. As Oscar Wilde famously said of the acquisitive rich, "They know the price of everything and the value of nothing." The truth is that we can't value and possess everything. Why should we want to? The real things in life that we value—friendship, home, community—are gifts that have to be chosen, earned, and sought out. We have to wait for them. Like planting an orchard, thriftiness is a prosperity that is planned and nurtured with the confidence that the future will soon be here.

There is no wealth but life.
—John Ruskin

Brooklyn House

When Simply New Is Thrifty and Fun

Who would think that building a new house and rental apartment in New York City could be thrifty and life-simplifying? Yet this townhouse, designed by a husband-and-wife team in a classic Brooklyn row-house neighborhood with affordable spaciousness and colorful flair, is an affirmation of the luxury of "enough." At only 1,800 sq ft., the main unit has enough room for a young family, with a soaring living room, three bedrooms, and a private garden.

Jill and John (an architect and a builder) decided to build a new house after studying the New York City real estate market. They worked out that building a new townhouse with a one-bedroom apartment for income was less expensive than buying into a co-op with high maintenance fees for

This New York City townhouse looks onto its own private backyard, a rare pleasure in the city. After a day at work, the owners enjoy the simple delights of the backyard terrace—barbecuing and an open-air dinner.

common areas, elevators, and staffing. They found an empty lot that provided the rare opportunity in the city to build a three-story house with a garage, a backyard, and a rental unit to help with cash flow.

The Row-House Challenge When you're building a row house, it's usually only possible to have windows in the front and back, and the only direction for expansion is straight up. Jill and John met the design challenge by staggering floor heights and level changes to bring in daylight and a tuck-under garage on the narrow lot. In the main apartment, the 13-ft. 6-in. ceiling in the kitchen/living area creates a sense of spaciousness and light even though the whole house is only 25 ft. wide with windowless sidewalls. Reaching the full height of the house, the garden-facing loft space is almost 23 ft. high. Sun from the garden-facing windows and three overhead skylights fills the kitchen/living room and spills into the master bedroom, which overlooks the living area like a tree-house balcony.

Open and airy spaces are a great luxury in the city, and for Jill and John, space and light trumped the need for expensive materials. Just by eliminating moldings, beds and tables fit right up against the wall to allow a greater sense of space. It's amazing how saving an inch or two can make a difference. Another space-enhancing strategy, the bathroom vanity and other built-ins "float" on legs to lend a sense of airiness within the minimal and compact floor planes.

→ With views and access to the backyard, the soaring living room is overlooked by the balcony of the master bedroom. Surfaces are flat with no moldings, which contributes to a simpler and more expansive-feeling space. The "Pool Party Blue" sidewall is a fun and thrifty way to bring color to a modern room with white ceilings and minimal detail.

→ → Overlooking the living room and backyard, the master bedroom is filled with light and color thanks to the whimsical repetition of simple squares: in this case, skylight, window, and peephole. In a house of white planes, the blue sidewall and wooden floors stand out as the essence of simple.

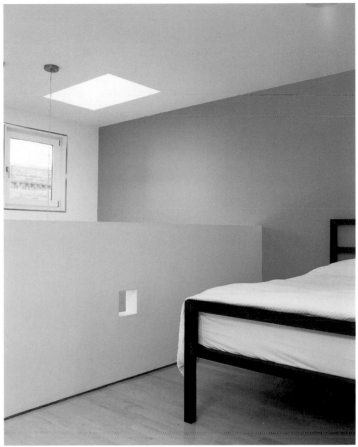

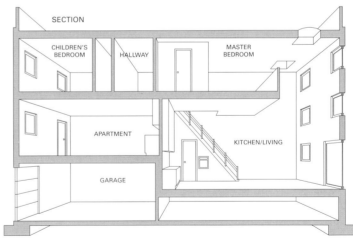

SECTION

CHILDREN'S
BEDROOM

HALLWAY

MASTER
BEDROOM

APARTMENT

KITCHEN/LIVING

GARAGE

Thrifty and Bold This townhouse skips fancy details, such as corbelled brick and elaborate cornices, that are often found on more costly new row houses. Yet, inside and out, the house has a unifying solidity and serenity that is expressed through smaller-scale details, metal reveals at material transitions, and whimsical colors and light metals. Less expensive than wood trim, the cold-rolled stainless-steel rails (made by an artist friend) and steel window reveals are a simple yet urbane option for conveying permanence and character. Another thrifty strategy throughout the house is the use of bright colors instead of expensive wall and floor coverings. And the house is filled with many standard, off-the-shelf cabinets that Jill and John bought at local home stores.

Thrifty and fun, the house is sparsely furnished yet vibrant, with changing textures of metals, masonry, and the angular custom-made light-metal stairwell that stands out against what Jill labels a "Dill Pickle Green" stair wall and simple white edging that accentuates the stair's diagonal form. The low-cost tactic of contrasting wall colors is a big part of this urban energy, with the green and "Pool Party Blue" tones extending the full height of the open loft space. In the bathroom, a grid of blue, white, black, and green tiles surrounds the mirror with a lively palette echoing the colors of both levels.

In the kitchen, the design of the stairs makes a bold statement with a triangle of wall accented by four simple cutouts: one for the oven, one for the microwave, one for a music system, and one for a door. What could be simpler? The marble

↑ Almost a piece of functional sculpture, the diagonal of the stair houses oven, microwave, and home electronics. The "Dill Pickle Green" wall stands out against the white and metal forms.
↓ Thrifty design makes use of every inch. The second-floor laundry doubles as a home office for late-night projects, wrapping presents, and other practical jobs that in larger houses are often spread over several rooms.
→ → Space is at a premium in this house, and clutter doesn't fit in with the simple aesthetics. One solution is a full-height pantry where large pots, plates, and the real stuff of cooking can be stored out of sight yet easily within reach.

backsplash contrasts elegantly with the black-and-white cabinetry, chrome hardware, and black dining table. Upstairs, an efficient layout with two children's rooms and a master bedroom with its own bath, closet, and built-in desk area offers a sense of privacy from the public main level.

At Home in the Neighborhood Jill and John's new house is the youngest kid on a block of red masonry buildings, yet the modern metal window surrounds and simple details complement the older neighbors. Modern yet respectful, this new kid fits into the street rhythms and scale with a three-part façade of red brick along with contemporary gray cement board accenting the center and the window surrounds. Composed with a careful balance, the façade's deep-set square and rectangular openings echo the rhythms of historic neighbors.

When they moved in, Jill and John had a huge garage sale because, with so many built-ins for books, seating, and storage, they didn't need much furniture. They are finding that they are only keeping the basic stuff. "If we're not playing with it, we donate it," Jill says of both toys and kitchen items. As part of a neighborhood with many young kids, Jill and John are also part of a neighborhood exchange for kids' toys and clothes.

Asked what they would do differently, both say they'd add another room for guests, as their house has become a popular stopping-off spot for friends and relatives. Fortunately, as part of the thrifty initial planning for the house, Jill and John had the foresight to design in the structural capacity to add a fourth story for a future guest room. Just one more room would make it a perfect house, but they love it the way it is now, and there is always the option of a roof garden regardless of whether they expand or not.

→ In the living room, furnishings are simple and spread out to celebrate the luxury of enough and the open flow of space. The composition of the green, white, and blue walls repeats the three-part theme of the windows.

FIRST FLOOR

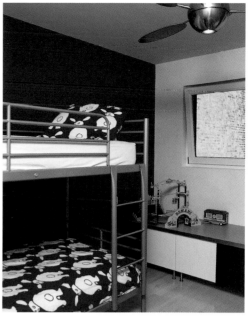

SECOND FLOOR

Simple Solutions Where Does All the Stuff Go?

For grown-ups, simple living in spare spaces can seem like freedom. But try telling a kid that the toys and toy box have to go. One solution in this house is the built-in toy bench that runs across the width of a child's room. Rather than buying another piece of furniture, this family acknowledged its storage needs in a multipurpose and space-efficient way. The secret, of course, is training the kids to put their toys away! An added feature is the bunk bed, which allows more room when space is tight.

Three Gables Are Just Enough

The Red Beach House

On the path to simplicity, we can learn a lot from weekend homes, where people shed many of life's obligations. Two hours and a beautiful ferry ride north of Seattle, Lopez Island has 2,400 permanent residents along with many seasonal visitors, like Peter and Betsy, who someday plan to make this verdant community their permanent home. Joe and Nancy Greene of Greene Partners, an architecture firm based on the island, designed this cottage in 1999 as a getaway home for the couple and their two school-age sons. In time, Peter and Betsy commissioned a more expansive compound up the hill (which we'll explore on pp. 218–225).

Borrowing from the tradition of Norwegian fisherman's cottages, the three red gables of this tiny cottage face the harbor. In casual beach-house style, the yard is left natural with a mowed area for walking and sitting.

Yet, the small, 1,150-sq.-ft. beach cottage is closest to the water and the nautical heritage of the island, set snugly to the harbor with a wizened old plum tree that frames the ocean view.

Perched on a gently sloping shoreline, this beach house draws on the Norwegian roots of *rorbuer*, or traditional red fisherman's cottages. A century ago, Norwegian immigrants brought their building traditions to these islands and bays, using the abundant local wood to create small homes with starkly simple interior and exterior walls. This unpretentious modern-day descendant, designed to meet strict codes for building size and location, is a delight of casual living. Here, weekend relaxation means clothes that hang on pegs (so no closets); comfy chairs pulled up around a woodstove (forget the "do-not-sit-on-me" antique chairs); and a dining table made of two old barn boards that sits at the heart of the kitchen in the center of the house. More than 200 years old, the table has knot holes and a textured patina that begs to be touched. No one bothers with drink coasters here; stains just add to the table's character. In a way, this simple gathering place serves as an expression for the hands-on texture of the entire cottage.

Sleeping, Dining, Living There's something fundamentally simple about a house divided into three parts, with three gables and three zones for living. Of the three gables, the one at the north end of the house serves as master bedroom, with two small kids' bunk rooms across the hall. Entry, kitchen, and dining areas fill the center, with the living room on the south end warmed by the woodstove. With the flexibility that's a hallmark of the simple home, the three gables are all connected, but the rooms can be closed off from each other with French doors between living and dining rooms and private doors to the bedrooms set off from the kitchen by a recessed hallway.

Backing up to the street, the mudroom and pantry are set away from the prime views yet are easily reached from kitchen and bedrooms. The mudroom couldn't be simpler: just two rows

← In the middle gable, the Scandinavian-inspired yellow door with herringbone planks provides a splash of color and relief from the vertical siding. The hutchlike storage units, which separate this kitchen/dining area from the mudroom beyond, are simply detailed with flush panel doors and finger pulls instead of hardware.

↑ Call it a mudroom or a row of pegs; hat and coat storage doesn't get much simpler than this.

↓ On the unassuming street side of the house, small four-pane windows flank the centerpiece yellow door. The minimal light fixture above the door is the only decoration on this front façade.

of pegs along the head-height walls that separate this room from the kitchen/dining room. Next to the mudroom, the pantry not only stores foodstuffs but also houses the refrigerator, an appliance with a vertical bulk that would overwhelm the clean lines of counters and table in the kitchen/dining area. With the refrigerator (and dishwasher) around the corner, the kitchen seems more like a ship's galley, with low cabinets that can double as serving counters.

Simple *and* Cozy? Coziness is something that many of us strive for in our homes. Traditionally, a cozy cottage was small and sparsely furnished, but today *cozy* has come to mean over-stuffed furniture, lots of throw pillows, and a warm color palette. *Simple* and *cozy* no longer seem to equate, with one implying a kind of austerity and the other plushness. Yet, true comfort arises from a well-designed space, not from its adornments. The rooms of this cottage, with their built-in beds, window seats, and cupboards, achieve coziness because of their human-scale proportions within the small confines.

Texture plays a big part, too. Inside, painted wood siding, white trim, and even the white bricks behind the stove come together in a simple layering that highlights the textures of wood and brick finishes. The wood siding is locally grown, vertical rough-sawn Douglas fir. During the design phase, the contractor warned the architect and owners that these relatively thin and unseasoned boards would warp—which was just the authentic effect they were hoping for! They liked the idea that the warping would create vertical lines of texture across the walls.

FLOOR PLAN

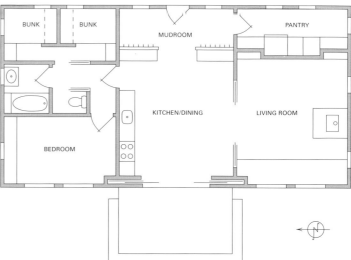

→ The built-in bench that runs the full length of the living-room gable is wide enough to serve as an extra bed. Drawers under the bench open with a simple finger pull, ready to store the clothes of overnight guests.
→ → Set against an all-white background, a couple of comfy chairs, an oriental rug, and a small woodstove are all it takes to warm up this intimately proportioned living room. Glass doors slide into the wall as a simple way to close the room off from the kitchen/dining area.

Traditional touches such as plain wall sconces, painted cabinets with finger-hole pulls, the wood-burning stove with brick hearth, and sliding barn doors create a harmony of simple functionality at many scales. With its monotone color palette, the house has a feeling of Shaker simplicity, but it seems a little rougher, as is perhaps appropriate for a home along a rugged shoreline. Rooflines are not quite so pristinely clean, the trim a little clunkier, proportions a little heavier without some of the ponderous seriousness of a perfected form.

Easy Living Comfortable to visit and easy to close up at the end of a weekend stay, the cottage is a getaway that doesn't demand a lot from its visitors. Practical details like the corrugated metal storm shutters on the water side, which can be folded down in the winter months, double as sun shades when they are open. Just inside the living-room window, built-in daybeds convert to sleeping beds with ample storage beneath. For privacy and quiet, sliding doors close off the living room from the kitchen and dining space.

The spare look in terms of furnishings means there is less to clean (and less to buy in the first place). And as Betsy says, there is no art on the walls because the views are so beautiful. In this modest beach house, all that is needed and no more makes for a human-scaled home, where the surprising luxury of less is more than enough.

→ With its views to the harbor, the master bedroom is a simple composition in white. The walls and ceiling are paneled with 1x8 boards, which have warped as expected (and desired). A built-in headboard holds what might otherwise clutter the top of a bedside table.

Simply Green Buy Locally, Think Globally
One of the simplest ways to "go green" is
to use materials and services that are available locally. For this house, the owners
used local craftsmen and as many local
materials as possible, a policy that helps
support the island economy while also
reducing the costs and energy used for
long-distance shipping. The frame of the
house is built with native Douglas fir, with
rough-faced cedar for the exterior siding
and fir for the floors. Local fir is also used
for the windows, made at a factory 60 miles
away. In the rush to find exotic building
products, it is easy to lose sight of what is
available right on your doorstep: local materials that can go a long way toward creating
a simple, authentic home.

A Farmhouse in the City

Simple and Accessible

For people who are physically challenged, even the simple act of coming downstairs in the morning or gardening can be an effort. Working with architect Rosemary McMonigal, Hans and Barb designed a remarkably healthy and accessible home where simplicity and long-term accessibility overrule extravagance. Standing tall in a neighborhood of bungalows and postwar capes, this two-story house evokes a farmstead grouping of buildings. Every detail, from the ramped entry to the elevator and the wheelchair-accessible bathroom, is designed to accommodate Barb's degenerative joint condition. The house is also designed to meet her chemical sensitivities to indoor air pollution from finishes and dyes.

Located in a city neighborhood and inspired by Barb's small-town Main Street childhood, the house adopts a farmhouse vernacular. The simple gable roof of the main house is connected by a shed roof over the ramp to the gable of the garage.

You would think that someone with physical challenges would want a one-story house. Why not avoid the expense of an elevator altogether? But for Barb, who is a master gardener committed to working outside, a healthy and simple life means having choices: She wanted a house where she could look down from the second story to her gardens and the street. She is challenging herself in a way that could never be possible in a traditional "accessible" apartment. Her house and gardens are not so much "easy" as they are therapeutic, inviting interaction with the outside, with neighbors, and with the seasons.

Healthy Choices A home to simplify your life is not just something that you buy in an architecture store, but the result of the hard work of making the right choices and resolving complex issues. Even in a house designed for someone with special needs, simple can mean spending (and consuming) less, as seen in the uncomplicated flat trim around all windows and doorways, low-maintenance tile and wood floors, handrails of steel water pipe, and off-the-shelf grab bars that double as towel racks.

The tools of accessibility can also be beautiful. Whereas access ramps are often seen as unattractive or as a tacked-on afterthought, this house's entry ramp and breezeway serve to bind the farmstead together, unifying house, garage, and screened porch. Both attractive and functional, the breezeway and ramp foster protected access to the garage, which is detached to isolate exhaust and oil fumes from the house.

For the interior, Barb spent two years working with her doctor to test products used in the house—from paint and adhesives to wood—with the goal of eliminating products and processes that compromise indoor air quality. The mechanical subcontractor even took all of the house's ductwork to a car wash to clean off the protective oils. They then had a final rinse with vinegar. Such tactics have vastly improved Barb's daily comfort and the energy that she can devote to her ongoing garden projects.

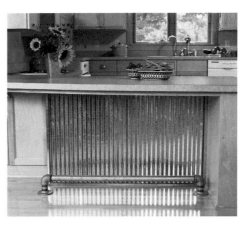

← The dining area in the one-room living area connects to the terrace with an accessible door and has windows with low sills for a better view of the garden. Fresh herbs for cooking are a few steps (or a short roll) out the door.

↑ The side of the kitchen peninsula facing the dining area has a deep knee space for pulling up a chair and resting your feet on the pipe rail. The corrugated galvanized metal at the back of the knee space picks up the rural farm aesthetic repeated throughout the house.

Simple Joys of Small-Town City Life Hans and Barb find simplicity through the old-fashioned idea of being part of a neighborhood where people don't hide behind walls and security systems. Directly above the living room, the master bedroom is filled with light on three sides and the garden views that greet the couple every morning. Indeed, every room in the house has windows on two or three sides for cross-ventilation as a simple response to Barb's chemical sensitivities. The rear-facing windows of their master bedroom and the living room don't have curtains. By good design and siting, Barb and Hans "own their views."

The master bathroom can also do without curtains because it is carefully screened by the garage roof. Besides creating "strategic privacy," well-placed windows can be a simple alternative to elaborate art and decorating. Years after moving in, Barb and Hans still have a box full of framed art because their home's abundant windows are landscape paintings in themselves.

This city farmhouse evokes the simple pleasures of Midwestern small-town life. The neighbors next door have three daughters who play in the shared backyard, where four galvanized-steel horse troughs glimmer in the lawn and sprout a rich collection of vegetables and herbs in summer. Beyond them, towering over the woods, soars a tall concrete grain elevator reminiscent of small towns on the plains. There is even an old galvanized-steel barn cupola sitting in the back garden.

Kitchen Solutions for Varying Heights More than just borrowing the galvanized-metal details of a farmstead, Hans and Barb really are living as urban farmers, growing as much of their food as possible and canning produce and drying herbs for the long Minnesota winters. Not surprisingly, they are active

---

→ A covered walkway leads from the main house to the screened porch, which is attached to the garage and enjoys a clear view of the garden. Behind the garage, galvanized metal watering troughs hold raised vegetable beds, while in the background, a grain elevator, icon of the Midwestern skyline, is a reminder that this urban farm is not far from its roots.

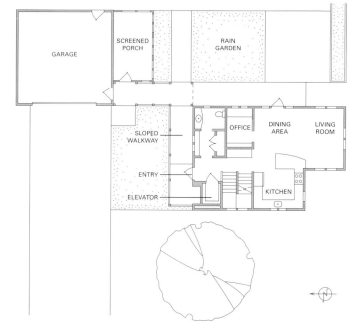

Simply Green Strategies for Indoor Health

For people with compromised immune systems, many of the petroleum-based products used in building materials can cause health problems and vastly complicate life. Most of us live with these effects unaware of them and their potential impact. The following are some key strategies for reducing contaminants, odors, and particles floating in the air:

- Eliminate/encapsulate construction products that off-gas volatile organic compounds (VOCs), such as particleboard and manufactured framing lumber.
- Use paints without preservatives or toxic tints.
- Choose finishes that will not trap dust; for example, use wood or tile instead of carpet.
- Isolate the garage from the house.
- Install an air-to-air heat exchanger with a high-efficiency particulate air (HEPA) filter that will clean the air and exhaust odors.

cooks, and, as in many simple homes, the kitchen lies at the center of the house, open to the living room and the front hall. One unusual complication is that Hans is 17 in. taller than Barb. To address this difference, McMonigal worked with the couple to design counters at two different heights so that each could work comfortably.

The stove and island are set into the lower counter level at 30 in., while the sink is located looking out the front window in the standard-height 36-in. counter. A cleverly designed pull-out step below the sink lets Barb easily reach the faucets. Like the rest of the house, the kitchen is wheelchair accessible with a 5-ft. turning radius. Light switches and cookbooks are set low at the end of the island, and cabinet sections are removable for future wheelchair access.

Overcoming Barriers to Life's Possibilities Barb looks at her house not as a response to her disabilities but as "a place for life's possibilities." She has simplified her life but at the same time kept it challenging. Beyond mere "accessibility," this richness of experience is the essence of Universal Design, a philosophy of design for public and private settings that stipulates that everyone, regardless of ability, should share experiences and choices of movement, entry, and views.

For this house, such choices mean that Barb can either walk up the stairs or take the elevator, depending on her condition on any given day. One of the experiences she savors is coming down the stairs in the morning to see what new flowers are blooming in the front-yard meadow. She has the choice, and for her, such options that many of us take for granted are the simplest essence of a life well lived.

→ Accommodating different needs is an opportunity for a good designer to turn potentially awkward into intriguing. Here, his-and-her sinks are set at different heights to accommodate individual preferences and wheelchair access.

↑ The counter at the sink is the standard height, but a pull-out step in the toe-kick space means that Barb can use it, too. The grille on the front of the step is the air supply grille for the kitchen.

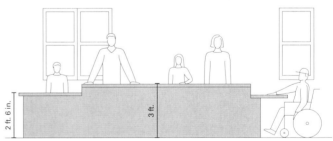

Simple in Spirit

California Cool in a Desert Climate

On the road to a simple life and a simple home, a number of destinations have a particular appeal—New Mexico, northern California, and the Florida Keys, to name but a few. When Gina first visited Taos, New Mexico, with her parents back when she was in college, she wasn't ready for the simple life. In fact, she hated the quiet pace of Taos. But today, she says of her adopted home, "It's simple here; it's quiet. The priorities are more intact." Clearly something changed in the interim—and it wasn't Taos.

After several years working as a graphic designer in San Francisco, Gina decided to get away from what she calls "the overnight express" culture and moved to Taos to find a

Tucked behind an island wrapped in corrugated metal, the colorful kitchen is the center of the home's activity. Bright red tiles, handmade by a friend of the owner, are a counterpoint to the wood and metal palette of the rest of the room, while the yellow painted wall behind the shelves is a thrifty way to add color.

less harried life closer to the land. Like many people who seek a simpler life in New Mexico, she needed to create her own job (in a place where there were few) and her own interpretation of "home" in a culture with centuries of architectural traditions. Today, she runs a gift shop with high-style design items and owns a passive solar house that reflects a taste for California cool in the high desert.

Adobe Modern   Gina moved to Taos because she craved less stuff, less worry, and less anxiety. Yet, she also wanted a house with modern energy, not a polite replica of the past. With the help of Ken Anderson and Pamela Freund of Taos-based EDGE Architects, Gina built a lively and fun two-bedroom house that has none of the pastel and pottery stereotypes associated with Southwestern décor. Instead, it's filled with salvaged school doors and kids' lockers along with unique lamps, dishes, and artwork carried by her store.

Built with locally made Rastra® blocks—concrete forms that use recycled polystyrene for high insulation value—the house's surface is plastered stucco to give the feel of a substantial adobe house. Yet, its tilted roof planes, shining brightly in the sun, are clearly something new.

A House of Two Wings   Sited to afford a long view of the canyon to the south, the house opens to the path of the sun in a dramatic angled shape where the metal roofs seem to float like bird's wings. Inside, recycled items such as a commercial dryer door instead of a laundry chute and metal school lockers instead of a front hall closet make you aware that this house has more than a bit of Santa Monica hipness in the desert. The front hallway is edged by an arc of corrugated galvanized metal that opens into the living room. This thrifty material also appears

→ A recent addition, the outdoor pergola/porch by the river is a favorite spot for family and friends to enjoy twilight dinners in the evening stillness.

Simply Green Design for the Whole Year
In a part of the world where the sun shines almost every day, solar design has to address the changing conditions of different seasons. This includes finding ways to harvest warmth, prevent glare, and avoid unwanted heat gain. As their first move in designing this passive solar house, architects Ken Anderson and Pamela Freund analyzed the relationship between window size and heat gain in the summer and winter seasons.

The house has three critical components: first, the big south-facing windows to admit winter sunlight; second, the thermal mass to store that heat in a concrete floor; and third, the overhang above the windows to block the sun in the hot summer months so as not to heat up the floor that provides passive cooling in the summer. Utilizing the seasonal sun angles, the architects designed the south-facing overhang to provide shade from the summer but not the winter sun.

around the kitchen and as innovative wainscoting for a kid's room. On the right, an "art nook" fills out the crook where the two angled wings diverge.

To the left of the entry, and oriented directly south, the master bedroom wing is a quiet place of retreat. Looking ahead into the living wing, you catch a glimpse of a large bank of south-facing windows and the stream-facing bump-out for the dining area. The whole living area opens up a few steps farther when you come upon a small kitchen—with counter, three skylights, and three stools—that is clearly a social hub for guests. The door from this social hub opens out to the pergola, which overlooks the canyon and river below.

An open office area lies at the center of the house with a large skylight above. In the future, this space can be closed off from the living area by adding a sliding barn door. Whimsy is definitely the order of the day here. In the playroom nook just off the office and living area, a kid-scaled elf door creates a magical portal into a secret room (actually a closet) that connects to the child's bedroom. Gina can work in the kitchen and keep an eye on her daughter, no matter where she is playing.

Ken proved to be a hands-on architect, helping Gina with such details as the concrete living-area floor that he painted using a bug sprayer. The floor's radiant-heat system is both very cost-effective during the cool desert nights and, according to Gina, allows for a wonderful and calming place to let a baby or toddler sleep. Ken observes that most people think they need a lot more space than they really do with good planning. He

↑ A secret door sized for a child connects through a closet into the daughter's bedroom. Built-in storage drawers under the daybed/window seat in the play nook are simply detailed and easily accessible.

↓ The palette of materials in the rest of the house continues into the child's bedroom, with a corrugated metal wainscot and walls painted a striking green. Simple touches like the star lights add to the whimsical effect.

→ → From the entry, the corrugated steel wall bends to the left to open up a view into the main living area with its soaring wood ceiling. To the right, a nook holds a playful collection of art objects

designed the house with Gina so that all of the spaces, even the heated floors, can take on multiple uses as places to walk, play, lounge, and sleep for young and old. Keeping the structure small at 1,650 sq. ft. and using standard sizes for walls and ceiling joists saved on construction costs.

Enduring Paths to Simplicity After many years in her desert home, Gina has come to realize that you don't always need to rush or spend a lot of money to find a better life. Rather, you have to find what "feeds your soul," and for Gina, that means a beautiful environment and bright colors. She prefers California cool and pop culture to chili peppers. Throughout the house, Gina displays framed advertisements for cars, bathroom fixtures, and food from the bright-graphic era of the 1940s and 1950s that go well with her colorful furniture, recycled school doors, and industrial materials.

Often the simplest solutions really do stand the test of time. They endure long after the fads disappear. Like a lot of Gina's décor, the ads are nostalgic for an era when the promise of modern living was novel and exciting. Fifty years later, her house takes the best of modernism—its quest for function, openness, and affordability—to find new paths for a simpler life in the desert today.

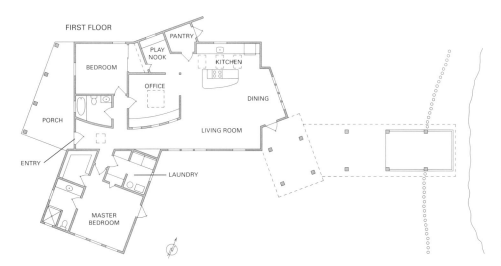

↑ Rather than formal and informal zones, this house has a main activity area and an "away" activity room tucked behind the corrugated metal wall. The away room does double duty as Gina's office.

Simply Green Recycle!

This playful desert home proves that you're never too old to go back to school. The owner and her architect had fun visiting architectural salvage yards, where they found a treasure trove of doors and lockers from postwar schools that had been remodeled or torn down. Classroom doors with varying milk glass patterns are reused and painted bright colors. Kids' lockers are put to new use as a front hall spot for guests' coats.

Sometimes, salvaged stuff can be born again in a completely unforeseen use. For example, the round window door of an industrial washing machine now fronts the clothes hamper in the connecting space between master bedroom and laundry. When the clothes pile up too high, they become visible as a nagging reminder that it's time for another wash.

Chapter Five Simple Is Timeless

Simple Is Always in Style How can you build a timeless and simple home when the world is moving ever faster? The answer lies in the questions that we ask. Throughout these pages, we explore stories of house building in which many kinds of people bring simplicity to their lives by asking what they really value in their homes and daily routines. Like stripping away the old layers of finish from an antique chair to reveal its essence, creating a simple home means finding your own essence, the daily rituals and special occasions that transcend changes in design fashions. For different people, the answers to the question "what is a timeless, simple home?" vary widely. But the fundamental questions that underlie building the simple home—How do I find comfort? What daily pursuits do I really value? What kinds of environments are healthful?—remain timeless.

Timeless Questions Every house is an expression of the technology and precedents of its time and culture. Throughout the history of residential architecture, there have never been truly "timeless" designs. But there have been what architect Christopher Alexander calls "timeless ways of building." We see this timeless spirit in the coherence of the New England village or the steadfast New Mexico adobe. These are houses and communities that grow out of the materials of the land and the spirits of the people who build them. They are true to their place and time, without pretense, allowing both visual consistency and room for variation.

Many historic homes respect the local climate and lend time-evolved wisdom to current styles. In the Florida home featured in this chapter, rooms opening off a center hall are breezy and windows are shuttered for cross-ventilation. Relying on this timeless way of cooling houses is a lot simpler than installing an expensive air-conditioning system. In a house in New Mexico, thick walls moderate the heat gain of sunny days in a timeless, simple solution to the hot climate.

Preindustrial builders often asked questions mandated by necessity. In a renovated Louisiana cottage, a copper bathtub occupies the center of its room, as it would have when servants filled it with pails. Even though the house now has plumbing, the tub stays in the center of the room. By evoking the necessary spaces of past functions, the copper bathtub stands as a special piece of memory that bridges the gulf of time.

The 18th-century Shakers left us a legacy of modest aesthetics grounded in practicality. Today, Shaker houses, chairs, textiles, and tools are striking in their elegant simplicity. Such historic roots inspire today's simple homes and how we furnish them. Our houses can have security and data systems within their walls while benefiting from past traditions in built-ins, ceiling heights, and windows placed for optimal daylight, heating, and cooling when the weather is hot.

Timeless Proportions Historic proportions refined over centuries and often shaped by the constraints of post-and-beam or adobe construction can be reborn with today's most advanced energy-saving and sustainable materials. In this section, we see timeless and well-proportioned spaces in the shaded courtyard of a house in southern New Mexico and the Creole wood traditions of the porch and gables of a house in Louisiana.

When the timeless questions of function and climate guide design, all sorts of new discoveries await us in crafting today's simple home. On Guemes Island, just off the Washington coast, a cabin built of industrial metal with a garage-door window expresses a deep understanding (and questioning) of modern materials, local climate, and how its owners want to spend time with nature.

Appropriateness rather than style is what matters here. When fashion becomes secondary, we can focus on the more enduring pathways to simplicity, including function, thrift, flexibility, health, and comfort. No matter how fast our world is changing, questions that get to the essence of life will never go out of style, nor will the houses that answer them.

There is nothing like staying home for real comfort.
—Jane Austen

Creole Simple

For some people, the search for a simple life and a simple home involves a journey back in time. But the challenge of living in a house built more than 150 years ago is finding a way to preserve its crafted character while making it work for today's necessities. Such is the balance that Madeline sought in her journey to restore an 1840s Creole cottage in Louisiana. She found a decrepit sharecropper house that had once accommodated tenant farmers on the Katie Plantation in Vermillion Parish. As her first step in adapting this house to meet her desire for a new home and a bed and breakfast, Madeline moved the building to Beaux Bridge, a town next to the famous Lake La Pointe bird sanctuary.

Built at a time before interior hallways were considered a necessity, the front porch serves as an exterior link between the main rooms. All the rooms in the old part of the house have French doors that open onto the porch.

The old South conjures images of tall columns supporting wide verandas of big white houses. However, not all southern houses are so elaborate, and some vernacular homes—those built by and for working people—offer ideal settings for a simple life. Abandoned for years, the Creole cottage had never been updated with running water or electricity. Some people might call such a place a shack, but Madeline saw the historic integrity and quality of its steeply pitched roof and high-ceilinged rooms. She found a beauty in its well-placed windows and wood structure.

In the back, she added a new wing made from reclaimed historic materials. With its porch recessed under the sloping roof, the front of the house doesn't have screens because they didn't exist in 1840. In those days and now, mosquito netting on beds has real purpose. The kitchen is updated to the 1950s with a large modern refrigerator concealed out of sight.

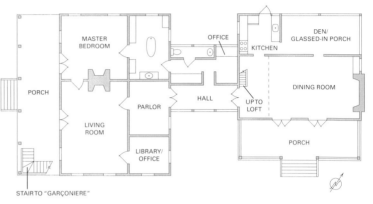

FIRST FLOOR

A House without Halls Madeline used to live in a new house in a new subdivision, but she disliked its open monotony and wanted a property that was more private. As an antique shop owner, she also frequently delivered furniture to new houses that seemed uncomfortable both as a place for the antiques and for the customers who bought them. She wanted a house with human-scale rooms, a real porch, and textured details.

As is typical of Creole design, the cottage has no interior halls. Madeline and her guests move directly from room to room or out the French doors along the porch that serves both as outdoor room and passageway. Because of the hot climate,

→ Recently added and made of old reclaimed materials such as brick and historic timbers, the kitchen porch is a working part of the house for shucking peas or enjoying an iced tea. A small formal garden in the foreground recalls French *parterres* that are composed of just green plants.

→ → Bare floors of antique wood, a beamed ceiling, and off-white walls extend the simple palette into the master bedroom. In that same aesthetic, the curtains are muslin and the bed is draped in mosquito netting, a timeless solution to an age-old problem in a time before screens.

the porch is an important room used whenever its breezes offer a respite from the heat; depending on the time of day, it can be a place for socializing, reading, or sewing. At the end of the porch, an elegant stair sweeps up to the attic bedrooms tucked under the gable. These rooms are called a *garçoniere* (from the French word for "boys"). Traditionally, the family sons slept up here. With perhaps a greater sense of oversight, the girls' bedroom lay at the heart of the main level, accessible only through the master bedroom.

Hybrid Cultures and Traditions Madeline's cottage offers a wonderful contrast of simple materials that frame both folk craft and elegant furnishings. Such a hybrid of periods, levels of elegance, and styles makes sense in this house. Creole buildings reflect Louisiana's rich roux of cultures, with French Creole, Anglo-American, and Acadian ingredients. Madeline's house is built with the French medieval construction technique of *colombage*, or half-timbered construction, infilled with *bousillage*, a material made of Spanish moss and local mud. The house also shows its Caribbean ancestry with an open porch and slender porch columns.

Built by local people with locally available materials, Madeline's house is simple in form and details on the outside yet rich in texture, color, and materials inside. This surprising contrast is one of the visitor's most memorable experiences. Opening the narrow French door into the living room, guests discover a beamed room of elegant mirrors, paintings, fabrics,

→ Entering the living room from the front porch, you walk into the simple comforts of the 19th century. Unfinished floors without rugs feel cool in the heat of the South, as do the muslin curtains at the windows. The beam-and-decking ceiling is preserved from the original 1840s house.

→ ↑ In the built-to-look-old kitchen addition, a steep ladder leads to a sleeping loft above. A glassed-in passageway connects the kitchen to the original Creole cottage.

→ ↓ This is a true French door, considerably narrower than what we call French doors today, with each door having eight panes of glass and a handle mounted lower than one would expect.

Simply Green A Sustainable Renovation

What appeals today as a sustainable strategy was often in the past just the best option. At the time this house was built, the lack of good transportation combined with a need to be thrifty and resourceful about using what was readily available inevitably led to sustainable construction methods. In Louisiana, southern yellow pine that grows locally and resists termites made beautiful flooring. Cypress, another local wood, is a durable material for framing lumber as well as for siding and many other uses. We have lost something of the authenticity of our local culture through the easy opportunity to buy whatever exotic product we wish.

For this house, the French medieval half-timber style of framing was adapted to Louisiana through the use of ginned Spanish moss blended with local clay to infill the walls between the cypress posts and beams (see the photo above). The brick used in the renovation was reclaimed and was originally made from the local clay soil. These simple country ways of construction prevailed because all materials were available locally.

porcelains, and furniture made with exotic woods. The living room combines the elegance of a New Orleans city home with the local craft and materials of the cottage's construction.

Lit by candles in the chandelier hung from the beamed ceiling, the living-room proportions speak to an earlier time. Here, the painted-wood country fireplace mantel is set beneath a traditionally French full-height mirror encased in a simple frame. Next door along the porch, the master bedroom remains where it was according to tradition, on the first floor. In one of the small rooms behind the master bedroom, originally referred to as a "cabinet," the bathroom focuses on a marvelous, free-standing copper tub in the middle of the floor.

What could be a better blend of past and current pleasures than sinking into a deep copper tub updated with hot running water? The toilet, which would not have been here in the 18th century, is concealed in a separate small room. Other modern conveniences, such as faucets and electrical appliances, are gracefully incorporated into the house out of sight. Light switches are hidden behind secret panels, air-conditioning ducts are below the floor in the crawl space, and electric outlets are mounted in the baseboard and painted out.

At the back of the house, the new wing has an old-fashioned kitchen with a dining table in its center and no appliances where guests gather for breakfast and at other times. The nearby working kitchen used for cooking has 1950s appliances: a refrigerator, stove, and sink with drain boards. It is close to the back porch, as it would have in 1840. Of all the places in the house, this porch, with its comfortable informal furniture and view of the kitchen garden, may be the most restful place to spend an afternoon with a novel and a glass of lemonade.

Madeline liked the idea that an old house is a home because life has been lived in it for generations. And in a region where good cooking, good friends, and shared history are valued, this is a home that offers all these simple pleasures so that visitors from far away can experience them today.

← Built of reclaimed brick, the kitchen chimney re-creates a simple country way of cooking with its built-in oven and wood storage. To the left of the chimney is a brick built-in counter that would originally have served as the kitchen counter with a peninsula for added workspace. Today it is a buffet for the dining table and chairs placed under the open hand-hewn rafters.

↑ The antique copper tub has been updated with plumbing, but it still sits in the middle of the bathroom, where it would have sat in 1840. A simple wall shelf holds towels and other bath necessities.

Timeless Modern

An Island House for All Seasons

Picture a simple "timeless" home, and it's unlikely that a modern green box clad in corrugated siding is the first image that springs to mind. For most of us, *timeless* equals *traditional.* But there's no reason a modern house can't be timeless as well. After all, timeless design is not so much about style as it is about a home crafted as a good fit for the site, the owners' needs, and the traditions of the region. Built as a vacation home for Laura and Bruce, an academic couple, this island house is both modern and "woodsy," depending, quite literally, on how you look at it. It's also a timeless place that will age gracefully in this moist and verdant land.

This island house is a contrast of new and old. Green corrugated-metal walls act like a Wild West storefront, essentially concealing a gable form. Inside, a warm wood interior glows in the early evening light. Both interior and exterior add up to a unified whole, an expression of how simple design can bridge the materials of many eras.

Designed by architect Robert Hull, the house unfolds as you move around it with very different front and end façades. The narrow ends are bookended by green rectangular metal panels that look a bit like old Wild West storefronts. Overlooking Puget Sound, the long front porch is a study in wood and glass, with carefully placed windows to make the most of views east to the mainland and mountains. From the entry path up the hill, the house nests into the land with a warm red face. On all sides, the landscape is intentionally left as a coastal forest, rich in moss and humidity.

Escape from the City In a house for two academics, you might expect to find tables piled with papers, periodicals, and buried books. But Laura and Bruce were adamant that they wanted an uncluttered getaway, so they just bring the books they need for the weekend. The owners were also adamant that they wanted a modest home, one where they could enjoy a simple lifestyle for several weeks of the year. As such, the house is barely 1,300 sq. ft., consisting of a long bar of a building for the living, kitchen, and dining areas and the master bedroom. Bob Hull took the list of rooms Laura and Bruce wanted and lined them up into a simple, slender rectangle sewn together by a long skylight at the roof's peak. The bedroom and studios open directly to the main room.

Facing the shoreline, a workroom doubles as a weaving studio and guest room with a pull-down bed and small bath. A roll-up garage door opens the entire east wall to water views with a deep overhang for protection from the rain. The workroom is a small but marvelous space with the feeling of a Japanese house when the screens are pulled back to let the forest in. Hull also talked Bruce and Laura into a covered front porch that has a view of Mount Baker. It's a fine place to sit as the rain gently falls, bundled up in blankets as if sipping tea on the deck of an ocean liner.

FLOOR PLAN

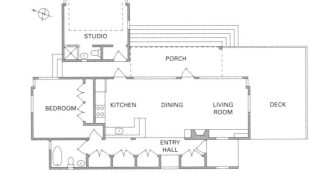

← ← In contrast to the open ocean-facing front of the house, the hillside façade, which is what a visitor sees first, is relatively unadorned. Hunkered down against the hillside, the window seat dormer looks out to the woods and the entry path.

← With hardly any paint or bright color, the living room is filled with daylight and the harmonious textures of wood. Windows on the east-facing wall reach from floor to ceiling for a simple effect without curtains or elaborate trim. The open corner window is a modern touch that complements the vaulted gable roof structure and central skylight along the roof's peak.

↑ In a part of the country where mosquitoes are not a problem, a rolling garage door opens up to provide a wondrous view of Puget Sound. The room is used as a combination studio/guest room.

→ → Sometimes the right furniture makes a room without walls. Set between kitchen and living room, the dining room becomes its own place thanks to the four-by-four pane square window and the perfectly scaled dining table set in front of it.

Simple Materials for Uncommon Effect Hiding behind the "bookends," the long living/dining room is a simple yet soaring space lit with a sliver of light from above. Bob Hull exposed the roof structure and standard 2x8 framing to create a rhythm of repeating patterns and spaces. The continuous skylight at the roof peak brings in sun from morning to late afternoon, and the light changes with the time of day and seasons, a remarkable feat in the dark coastal forest. Like the corrugated-metal exterior, the skylight is a standard industrial product made of double-thickness acrylic panels bent over the wooden frame.

The long east-facing deck is built with Trex® decking, an eco-friendly material combining recycled plastic and wood that is impervious to moisture and doesn't get slippery in the rain. Along with the contemporary industrial and recycled materials, the house uses local woods such as cedar for the exterior battens and hemlock for the trim. In all, the house is an expression of timeless regionalism at its best, combining modern and traditional in a Northwest vernacular of openness: light with bountiful amounts of wood.

Design for All Seasons Designed as a summer house where Bruce and Laura might one day retire, this small house exudes flexibility for all of life's and nature's seasons. Built on one level and entirely accessible, the house works for everyone from a 95-year-old aunt who comes to visit to children who can run up and down the hillside paths.

Timeless design also means durability throughout the seasons of the year, a true test of materials and waterproofing in the rainy and windy Northwest. The challenge of keeping natural materials such as wood dry in a rain forest environment is solved in this cabin with a double wall that allows airflow and dries out what might otherwise cause rot. The forest green

→ Part of the delight of this house lies in its creative use of doorways, as seen here in the sliding door that opens a vista through the studio wing. The deck is made of recycled wood and plastic fibers, a product known as Trex.

metal panels and roof are protected with a Zactique® finish, frequently used by Northwest architects to reduce long-term maintenance. And with no need to paint the industrial-strength corrugated-metal siding or the wooden interior, this is a low-maintenance home for the owners, so Laura and Bruce can spend their time as they please, reading books and walking the rocky beach.

With generic names like House #5, many modern houses have a deserved reputation for being impersonal and uncomfortable. Yet the best of modern ideals, such as contemporary materials and corner windows, can lend a sense of timelessness to simple homes. Such is the story of this cabin, a home that grows out of its site with indigenous and industrial elements. It's a modern vernacular: place-specific and timeless with simple yet perfectly scaled walls, porches, and rooflines. This is a house beyond fashion, a home with the enduring quality of a well-laid-out plan that works for all ages.

↑ The roof-peak skylight is framed with smaller-dimension lumber, a sustainable strategy for reducing the need for old-growth timber.
↓ The house overlooks Puget Sound with floor-to-ceiling windows and old-fashioned Adirondack chairs. The three-part door that lets in maximum light is an inventive update of a traditional Dutch door.
→ → The back wall of the living room has the feel of a traditional rustic cabin, with floor-to-ceiling wood planks, built-in bookshelves, and an inviting window seat. On cold nights, the fireplace makes a warm backrest for reading a good book.

Simple Solutions Tucking In a Window Seat
Set between a pair of storage units that line
the back hallway, this window seat is an ideal
place to escape for a quiet read. Updating a
timeless tradition of comfort, the dormered
nook is perfect in proportion, light, and function. With an intimate view of the hillside, the
asymmetrical window pattern echoes the
end windows in the living room and master
bedroom; one large pane opens for ventilation. The space is small, the lamp and cush-
ion disarmingly simple.

The Courtyard House

Learning from the Past

For Carolyn and Joseph, finding a place to build a new home was a chance to simplify their lives by reconnecting with the landscape and vernacular building history of New Mexico. In the southern high desert of New Mexico, they found a 10-acre site next to a small stream nestled in a cool valley. Their house makes use of time-tested solutions for flow-through ventilation and solar exposure to optimize comfort and connection to the outdoors through all seasons.

In preparing to move from Ann Arbor, Michigan, the couple interviewed local architects to find someone who really understood the history of New Mexico's building traditions. In the end, they hired Jon Dick of Archaeo Architects

Nothing says "simple home" louder than a gable wall pierced by two timeless windows bathed in the evening glow. The open door leads into a courtyard through a covered walkway or *zaguan*.

in Santa Fe, who more than any other candidate clearly grasped the importance of site topography and outward views to such regional landmarks as the majestic Sierra Blanco visible miles to the north.

No matter where you build, it makes sense to find out where the original people lived, where the historic paths and trade routes were. After all, without the benefit of modern technology and transport, they had no choice but to find the simplest solutions for access, heating, and safety. In New Mexico, the Indians, Spaniards, and later Anglo settlers built and traveled along the rivers and in low, protected places, contrary to conventional real estate wisdom today that emphasizes 360-degree views from the tops of mesas. Whereas a traditional Midwestern house turns outward with porches and large windows to catch breezes, a high desert house turns inward to avoid the dusty winds of summer and winter cold. Since ancient times, desert houses have focused on courtyards, one of the simplest solutions to creating a cool and sheltered microclimate. In the winter, the low sun streams under overhangs and into the south-facing sheltered courts to heat up thick walls that radiate heat into the night.

The Drama of Entry Joseph and Carolyn had lived in Japan for three years, where they came to respect the subtle textures and shadows of traditional Japanese homes and gardens. As with a Buddhist temple, the courtyard house is reached through a series of entrances: first, a long view from the grass-and-stone entry path, then a center-folding old Mexican door serving as a gate, then a shady pass-through under the roof, and finally, the

→ The simple symmetry of the ceiling beams is repeated in the tiny windows and in the double-hung windows at eye level, which are set deeply to accentuate the thickness of the walls. Traditional Mexican tiles make a cool and easily maintained floor.

→ → Columns of peeled oaks felled from the site run around the three sides of the courtyard. The deep overhangs not only provide shade but also serve as the corridors of the house. Huddled next to the wall, the table and chairs cling tenaciously to the available shade.

Simply Green Built to Last

Local precedents are often the simplest and most cost-effective guides for material selection. Inspired by the example of Fort Stanton, a cavalry fort a few miles downriver, the owners chose a pitched standing-seam metal roof appropriate for the extremes of climate, ranging from blazing sun to heavy, wet snowfalls.

Once used because it was a durable and easily shipped material, metal still makes sense for roofs today. Unlike the 30-year asphalt shingle roofs common throughout suburbia, metal roofs can last up to 100 years. Even though they initially cost more to install, metal roofs offer an ease of maintenance and a life cycle that are far more thrifty in the long run. And from an environmental standpoint, they can be recycled for new uses so they're not taking up space in landfills.

porch, or *portal*, that wraps the courtyard on three sides. You then arrive at the home's weathered front door, which was salvaged from a Mexican convent. This measured sense of arrival, with its syncopation of sun and shade and the anticipation of daylight at the house's heart, creates a simple drama for visitors in a way that towering gables or elaborate lighting never could.

Re-creating the built-to-last simplicity of beloved historic buildings requires more than assembling a kit of parts. In this house, the feel of old New Mexico adobe houses is conveyed through Jon's knowledge of the indigenous scale and proportions of vernacular and folk houses. Surrounding the courtyard, or *placita*, the rooms are a comfortable 15 ft. wide with windows opening on both sides to the surrounding hills and to the protected court. This narrow width of the rooms is a holdover from what was structurally possible in a traditional adobe house in which mud bricks supported a flat wood-beamed ceiling.

The house conveys a monastic simplicity of connected rooms with few hallways. You see where you are going at every turn. Yet, all of the rooms—from the bedroom wing to the library at the northwest corner of the house—retain a distinct identity and privacy to be found simply by closing one of the 12 interior doors that the couple recycled from a historic storefront building in Michigan. At roughly 2,500 sq. ft, the house's sense of spaciousness is fostered by varied ceiling heights and internal room connections that culminate in carefully framed window views. Ceiling heights range from 8 ft. to 18 ft., all in a graceful proportion to the width of the rooms. Thick walls evoke the silent daytime coolness of old adobes.

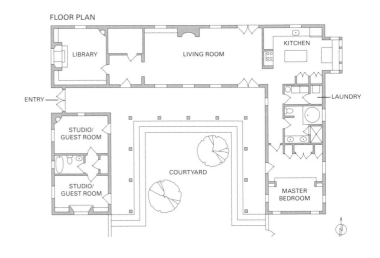

FLOOR PLAN

→ Only 15 ft. wide, the living room feels intimate with a fireplace and windows on two sides. Because of its narrow width, winter sun reaches across the room, with the light coming in the southern windows moderated by the porch on the courtyard side in the summer. The ceiling of *vigas* (log rafters) and decking is traditional adobe construction.

→ → In the vastness of the Southwestern high desert, an alcove with an arched ceiling for the bed feels cool and protected. Deeply recessed windows with splayed sides reflect the shimmering desert light.

Do It Yourself Joseph and Carolyn sorted through the general contractor's bids to try to figure out which projects they could take on themselves as a cost-saving measure. Often, certain finishing work is outside of the critical path of construction and well suited to dedicated home builders. They hand-rubbed century-old doors salvaged from Mexico, stained terra-cotta floors with colored beeswax, and installed 6,000 bricks to pave the courtyard steps and walkways. Joseph hand-carved several oaks felled for the house into columns around the *portal*. They were the only large trees removed for the project; for a house built to last, it makes sense that they should live on.

Joe and Carolyn's labor has clearly paid off. The long living room, with its textured walls and warm tile floor, recalls the great hall of a Spanish-Mexican hacienda centered on furniture grouped around the fireplace. Along the top of this tall room, clerestory windows serve multiple functions: They admit breezes during the hot summer months while bringing ambient light into the living room that would otherwise remain dark in the shadows of the *portal*.

The Payoff of a Simpler Home Carolyn and Joe are just now beginning to reap the benefits of "jumping off the cliff" into a new life appropriate to a new land. They have made a great initial investment of time and care in lasting regional materials and time-tested design. Carolyn compares the hidden layers of complexity and hard work that went into building their house with learning how to ride a horse, a graceful journey that seems free and easy to the casual observer, yet is actually far more complex. "The things that look the most simple and effortless in life," she observes," actually take the most practice."

↑ A *kiva* fireplace set into the corner of a room (here, the library) is a traditional feature in an adobe house. In keeping with tradition, the fire is built with split logs on end leaning up against each other.

→ → Blending their Japanese sensibility with the New Mexico countryside led the owners to value the "Zen view," a raised window seat in a thronelike alcove in the library that focuses on the majestic Sierra Blanco range.

Eat In, Eat Out In traditional New Mexico adobes, you either eat outside on the *portal* or under the trees on a long harvest table. When the weather is less kind, extended families often eat inside at long tables in the open living room. Joe and Carolyn's kitchen is the spiritual heart of their house, serving as a living and gathering place. An intimate dining alcove surrounded by windows on three sides invites you to take a seat and linger. It's also a nice counterpoint to the elevated window seat at the other end of the house. For grander occasions, the formal dining area at the east end of the living-room area opens directly into a stand of oaks on the hillside. On warm nights, the screened French doors at both ends of the table create the effect of dining in a pavilion.

Gulf Coast Simple

White on White on White

You'd expect a stay on the Gulf Coast of Florida to be casual and relaxing, yet so many of the winter homes along the coast are fancy and formal, not at all conducive to bare feet and slamming screen doors. But this house on the banks of the Apalachicola River fits the informal mold, a stripped-down, unpretentious home that invites you to brush the sand off your feet as you step onto the porch after a day at the beach. The porch leads through the front door into a traditional wide center hall that extends to the back of the house, encouraging gentle breezes to flow through the house when the doors are open at both ends.

In the master bathroom, a pedestal sink fills a dormer on the back side of the house. White-painted beadboard ties together the dormer, knee walls, and ceiling in a strong, simple statement.

The renovated 19th-century house is elegant in a simple kind of way, both historic in its symmetrical floor plan and modern in its open kitchen and dining area. As the author of several cookbooks, the owner, Jane, is a fan of this sort of balance in home and food. For her, simple food and simple architecture both look effortless yet actually grow out of careful planning.

Remodeled with Restraint Originally built across town in 1870, the house was moved to this site overlooking a 200-acre nature preserve between the town shrimp-boat harbor and the Apalachicola River. When Jane found the house it was a little worse for wear, but she fell in love with its historic and humble character. Part of the appeal was the utilitarian horizontal wood beadboard on many of the inside walls, as well as the absence of all but the most basic trim and moldings. The graceful proportions of the rooms with their 12-ft. ceilings evoke the practical solutions of the time before air conditioning, where tall ceilings allow the hottest air to rise and cooler air to settle at sitting level.

Southern in style, the hipped roof and white-columned porch owe a debt to French Caribbean Creole architecture. From the outside, the tall double-hung windows are symmetrically arranged, as was the fashion in 1870. Inside, the rooms accommodate the exterior classic order of the windows with pleasing square (or almost square) proportions. The symmetry of the

→ Relaxing on the porch is an official activity on the Gulf Coast, and the rockers are always ready outside this renovated 1870 home. From the porch, a boardwalk leads to the shrimp harbor and the Apalachicola River's outlet into the Gulf.

→ ↑ Tall floor-level double-hung windows that open onto the porch are a traditional feature of 19th-century southern homes. This modern-day interpretation is in the living room.

→ → The remodeled home retains the feeling of a time when rooms were rooms and open floor plans were yet to be invented, yet it seamlessly incorporates such modern touches as the built-in egg-crate bookcase in the corner of the living room. The couch and chairs were designed by the architect and made of cypress reclaimed from the nearby Apalachicola River

FIRST FLOOR

floor plan and classic proportions of the rooms are strong enough to hold their own alongside such modern updates as the kitchen and fireplace wall.

Southern Comforts From the rear deck, the back door opens directly into a kitchen set up for serious cooking. Storage is located under the counter or in the pantry wall that covers one entire side of the room. Without the need for upper cabinets, the kitchen work area feels open and luxuriously uncluttered. The white and minimal kitchen base cabinets quietly blend into the larger room that also serves as a dining area for the house. Across the rear deck from the kitchen there's a small pavilion with two rooms, just far enough away to make the office feel separate from the house and to give the library the feel of a retreat.

The rear deck also gives entry to the back door of the center hall. In today's world of standardized new home floor plans, this hall might seem large, even wasteful of space. However, its elegant proportions and the graceful way it connects the rooms aligned along each side make it the dramatic focus of the house. Its cool, empty interior gives all the rooms the luxurious feel of space. The stairway off the central hall is recessed into the sidewall, quite a change from the attention-grabbing stairs that swirl up to the second floor of many homes built today.

With its view of the harbor, the living room feels cool and serene in its restrained elegance. In his classic style of paring down what exists to the essentials, architect Hugh Newell Jacobsen designed the renovation to balance the room's historic proportions with modern features such as the floor-to-ceiling bookcase that emphasizes the room's height. The wood

---

→ Although this is the kitchen of a professional cook, it purposefully has the feel of a home kitchen. With a restrained white palette and no-nonsense stainless hardware and trim on the appliances, this is a simple, modern look in a traditional home. The polished old heart pine floor provides a warm contrast with the otherwise all-white room.

Simple Solutions Pull-Out Pantry

In a cookbook author's kitchen, which doubles as teaching space for cooking classes, functional storage is a top priority. But without upper cabinets, where do you put all your pots and pans? The clever solution in this remodeled kitchen is an entire wall of built-in storage, 30 in. deep to provide room for every imaginable kitchen item. The generous storage provision includes a pull-out pantry that's invisible when slid back into the wall. With matching horizontal beadboard panels, the oven and refrigerator also blend seamlessly into the storage wall. Only their ventilation louvers and handles show.

paneling on the face of the fireplace wall is horizontal bead-board that back in 1870 would have been considered a poor man's decorating solution. Today, we appreciate it as an inexpensive and eloquent wall finish. In this modern interpretation of historic character, the fireplace mantel, deep baseboard, and ceiling crown molding provide the feel of authenticity with modern restraint.

Across the hall from the living room and kitchen are two bedrooms and a small bath. Entering the house, you would hardly know these rooms were there until you come through the openings off the hall to discover them. Spare and minimal in size, the bathroom tucks behind the stair in the available space. Respecting the geometry of the old house, it is a beautifully simple way to fit modern conveniences into an existing structure.

Upstairs, the master bedroom and bath occupy the entire vault of the hipped roof, remodeled from the attic of the original 1870 house. With dormers on all sides, the rooms command the views of the shrimp harbor, nature preserve, and river beyond. Understated in its design, the bedroom is all that is needed and no more: the essence of a simple home.

Simple Food, Simple Home In cooking as in home design, the seemingly simple recipe can actually be harder to follow than a more elaborate one. Ironically, it takes a lot of knowledge to do things that look simple. Good cooks who are experts at

↑ Borrowing a stripped-down aesthetic from island houses, the airy entry hall is the epitome of simple. The wooden chandelier provides a glimmer of ornamentation, but even this fixture continues the white-on-wood theme.

↓ Referencing the Greek Revival roots of the front door and its sidelights, this new mantel is eloquent in its stacking of moldings, introducing an elaborate detail in contrast with the simple elegance of the horizontal beadboard that frames the fireplace.

→ → The understated, enclosed wood-paneled stair winds up to the attic bedroom. The treads on the steps are reclaimed old heart pine, used in the original house as baseboards.

delicious and simple fare have matured through the gussying-up phase of using too many ingredients for a muddy outcome. Architects who are masters of understatement have moved beyond complexity and contradiction to distill down the pieces of complex problems. In this renovation, the essence of the original historic house lies in its room proportions, porches, and multipaned windows with their shutters. Jane's Gulf Coast house is a timeless classic that required subtle flavors for its updates to meet the needs of new and old. Her renovated home doesn't shout at the neighbors; it's pared down to the play of light and shadow on white and wood.

In the introduction to one of her cookbooks, Jane writes: "I cook for myself because I like to eat well. I also want to prepare economical meals that are good for me and are centered around seasonal food. It's as simple as that." In her single life, solving the complexities of going solo in the kitchen has gone hand in hand with enjoying the simple pleasures of life—good friends, fresh air, fresh food, and a house that's not quite as simple as it first appears.

→ Finished in drywall, the upstairs bedroom has a lighter, more modern feel than the rooms downstairs. Dormers on three sides fill the vaulted space with light; the front dormer is a door opening onto a tiny balcony overlooking the harbor.
→ ↑ On the main level behind the stair, a narrow hall connects the two downstairs bedrooms. The simple, restrained palette of the rest of the house—stained, polished floor and white-painted beadboard—continues into these semihidden rooms.
→ ↓ Simple home and simple food come together at the kitchen table, where the owner delights in serving friends a home-cooked meal. The 1940s-era poster (one of several in her collection) brings a rare splash of color to the simple white color scheme.

Chapter Six Simple is Sustainable

A Green Aesthetic Many simple homes are also sustainable. But what does sustainable building really mean today? Sustainability is about finding the right balance between needs and resources for the long term. To ensure this balance for our children and our children's children, we have choices about how much we use today. Sustainability isn't only about yurts, composting toilets, and green gizmos. And it's not just a dreary necessity. Sustainable living and design is an opportunity to be in tune with the simple pleasures of nature. More than basic energy efficiency, simple is a green aesthetic that provides the most basic pleasures of life—simple sounds, daylight, and fresh air.

In lives that are increasingly disconnected from nature, a green aesthetic is a chance to make a connection with nature in the backyard and in the region. What's preferable: a constant indoor air temperature with the noise of a heating and air-conditioning system fan or the delight of hearing bird calls coming in on the breeze through open windows? Elaborate materials imported from foreign shores have their place, but local materials bring the spirit of the place inside in ways exotics never can. Local wood and stone are the essence of a locally rooted green aesthetic.

Commonsense Solutions Sustainable design has become a trendy concept, when really it is as old as the hills. Old commonsense strategies that can be designed into a home with proper planning, such as natural daylighting and ventilation, can and should be part of every simple home. Daylighting strategies reduce dependence on electric lighting, prevent unwanted glare, and decrease air-conditioning loads. Natural ventilation and fresh air reduce dependence on mechanical systems that are most often run by fossil fuels and electricity. These simple, sustainable strategies make a difference in terms of environmental impact, but they don't have to add to the construction cost.

There are many everyday solutions to green dilemmas. Often options like wind generators sound tempting but are not the best real-world choices. Understanding your local natural resources and what is scarce in your region is a much better first step. In Minnesota and Illinois, energy is imported and in demand due to the climate. In California, water is scarce. Saving energy in the upper Midwest and saving water in California are green priorities.

Saving Energy In hot climates that demand a lot of energy for home cooling, energy efficiency is the most important step you can take to reduce impact on your region and on the planet. The same is true for very cold regions. A simple and effective path to energy efficiency is adding insulation and proper ventilation to your new or remodeled house, which will give you a payback in real dollars. Adding a high-efficiency furnace also can have a reasonable payback. Payback means that you will recapture your up-front investment in terms of reduced monthly energy costs within about three to five years.

The three houses in this section demonstrate different ways to save energy in simple ways: an energy-efficient building envelope, taking advantage of shading available on site, and high-efficiency mechanical equipment. The house in Chicago is fitted for the future upgrade of built-in filters on selected windows to allow filtered natural ventilation. In many houses today, windows are all located on one side of a room, leaving dark areas at the far side. The result is that you need to shut the shades and turn on the lights. Even in temperate seasons and climates, many homes pass the day all closed up. All three of the houses in this section, located in temperate as well as rigorous climates, take advantage of natural daylight and fresh air.

Simple sustainable is born of caring; it is not measured in tons of waste or board feet of lumber. It is not just a certain product that looks good. It is doing what you can do with what you have and creating beauty in your home that you get to live with as a part of your own willingness to care.

Wherever you live is your temple if you treat it like one.
—*Buddha*

North Shore Cabin

Walking Lightly on the Land

The old cabin perched precariously on the rock ledge. With only 5 ft. of counter in the small kitchen, the 1947 structure was a remnant of a less lavish time when going "up North" was a much simpler and more rustic adventure. Medora, the new owner, found this modest cabin along Lake Superior's dramatic North Shore, surrounded by five acres of birch forest, rocky cliffs, and a stream that flows into a sheltered cove. Offering wraparound views of the lake and up the shore, the cabin needed to be completely rebuilt for comfortable year-round use. In addition, Medora's directive to my architectural firm included the charge to explore innovative strategies for sustainable building and energy conservation.

In a compact house, vertical space is used cleverly to convey a sense of spaciousness and views through to the ceilings of the bedroom beyond. For this efficient main room to work, two of the cabin's four chairs live in the bedrooms and are brought into the living room as needed.

Although this remodel is far-reaching in its list of green goals, many of its strategies are simple to achieve. Medora preserved the modest spirit of the original home as a sustainable model for today with coziness and efficiency in a small space. Storage is very limited, with pegs behind the front door instead of a mudroom or even a closet. The luxury of enough in this cabin is all about making sure that nothing gets in the way of experiencing the wonderful rocky shore.

The Simple Sounds of Nature What strikes you most when you come in from the outside is the silence of the cabin: There's no whirr of a heating system or mechanical hum of an air-conditioning fan. If you hear a noise, it's more likely to be the trill of a bird call coming in through an open window.

Fresh air and sunlight are this getaway's most basic pleasures. The cabin breathes with the seasons; its natural ventilation strategies provide comfort with little or no energy. Designed to admit light at all times of day in all seasons, the cabin has windows that open without creating drafts, ensuring a quietness that allows the natural sounds of birds and the waves to be heard inside. Many people think they need a weatherized sun porch to enjoy the sun, when in reality they can have an entire house that is naturally lit. In this cabin, the changing light day by day and over the seasons is a simple reminder of where you are.

A simple home isn't all about white walls and flat ceilings; it can also be a home with a curved ceiling wrapped in knotty pine. One of the simplest things you can do to build sustainably is to use a few local materials. The wood used in the interior of this cabin is all recycled and includes some from the demolition

→ Light from the clerestory windows flows down the curved wooden ceiling into the mistress bedroom, which recalls the inside of a boat hull. The custom fish hinges on the cabin doors were made by a local sculptor.

Learning Simple from the Past Like many sustainably designed houses, this tiny cabin updates simple and sensible folk building traditions. The cabin pays homage to the settler history of its site with a curved roof, the interior ceiling of which is finished with shiplap siding that echoes the boat hulls of the former fishing village nearby. Its spaces are faithful to the contours of the original rooms, as are its knotty pine walls. And in the serenity that is rediscovered here, the voice of nature comes through loud and clear.

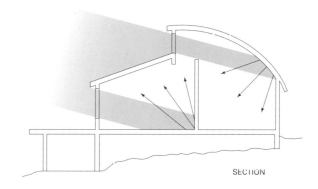

SECTION

of a nearby maintenance building from a long gone logging company. Also sourced locally, the kitchen and bathroom granite comes from a nearby quarry. Together, the wood walls and granite surfaces evoke the balance of the rocky shore and northern forest outside. On cold nights, the wood creates a soft and warm feeling. In summer, the smooth granite is a cool surface for leaning against while gazing at the forest.

All That You Need In less than 1,000 sq. ft., this cabin has two bedrooms and all that is needed for a comfortable stay. If you're looking for a big-screen television, you won't find one here. In multipurpose efficiency, the only table has drop leaves and can be opened when guests come over or accommodate just one as a worksurface with a swinging light anchored to the kitchen island. As this is a retreat from the city for Medora, she considers its limited storage an asset of its "cabinness," where life is simple and unencumbered with the stuff of everyday life. Storage is limited yet strategically designed to minimize any kind of barrier between visitor and lake. The kitchen has no upper cabinets, just basic shelves for art and a small collection of crockery for daily use. In each of the bedrooms, a small closet provides a bit of hanging space for clothes and a place to store chair cushions and a vacuum (cabin stuff that typically requires a room or garage of its own).

Sometimes a small investment of space can make a big addition to comfort and to connection with the landscape. Early on, Medora and I decided that one bathroom was enough and

---

→ Providing all the pleasures of one-room living, the cabin is shipshape in its efficiency and accommodates relaxing, projects, dining, and cooking. All surfaces are paneled in knotty pine, even the refrigerator, which is built in with a wood cabinet to look like it's part of the cabin walls. Up high and facing south, clerestory windows wash light down on the bookcases and open for summer ventilation.

→ → In a small cabin, the luxury of a great view from the bathtub is an unexpected surprise. The tub surround and floor tiles were made by local artisans to match the granite and have imprints of Lake Superior fish in them.

FLOOR PLAN

that the bathtub needed a lake view; with that in mind, a mere 3-ft. addition did the trick. The resulting bathroom soars up to the sky with a 17-ft. curved ceiling and two tall windows that look out to the lake.

Living Lightly on the Land Living sustainably is a perspective on time that does not borrow resources from the future and means living responsibly today. How does that work in simple, practical terms? Energy efficiency in this cabin started with reducing the need for heat to one-fifth of that required by a typical house the same size. To accomplish that, the house was fitted with an added layer of insulation on all walls, ceilings, and the foundation, as well as with high-insulating-value windows.

Medora's cabin not only saves energy, it also generates energy. A new garage houses the renewable electrical generating system, its roof covered with photovoltaic panels. Nearby, a wind generator whirls at the edge of the cliff. Although the renewable energy generating system itself is complex, its goal is simple: self-sufficient energy. Powered by sun and wind, it reduces the pollution caused by the mining and burning of coal, the primary local energy source.

Simple green design is not all about fancy technologies. It's about being where you are, building with local materials, and using fresh air and daylight. Although this cabin has some sophisticated energy systems such as the wind generator, it's simple in its green aesthetic, with local woods, the sound of wind, and the feeling of being connected with an ancient site.

→ The remodeling of the cabin relocated the stove to the lake side of the room, so that anyone sitting on the couch has a view up the shore with a fire in the foreground.
→ ↑ Built of half-log siding typical of the 1940s, when the original cabin was constructed, the interior of this new wood shed is made from dead birch trees harvested on site.
→→ ↑ Inspired by the steel railings on a ship, the deck and stair railings were fabricated in a shipyard in Duluth. In a subtle reference, the shape of the uprights repeats the shape of the bathroom window.

Simple Solutions Simple Green Aesthetics

Restraint is a basic part of the green aesthetic of this cabin, providing abundance without excess. Here, the space-heating and hot-water systems are tucked under the deck so that their mechanical sounds do not intrude on the stillness of the cabin. Accomplishing this had its complexities, but the result is the simple luxury of stillness that allows the sound of rustling leaves to be audible through open windows.

In the north woods, a rare summer day will approach 90 degrees. The comfort of air conditioning for this cabin is provided strategically rather than by a conventional air-conditioning unit. The simple strategy in this case is a well-insulated shell that keeps the interior space cool and comfortable if windows are closed before the day heats up. Then in the evening, when the heat of the day is past, the simple act of opening both the clerestory and regular windows invites in the refreshing evening breeze.

Framing and finish wood for the cabin and garage came from a sustainably managed forest and sources of recycled wood. And the copper roof, a reminder of ore deposits on a nearby island, will not have to be replaced for well over 50 years.

A Sonoma Farmhouse

Sustaining the Best of New and Old

"Green" and "sustainable" are concepts that people often associate with modern buildings and contemporary, high-tech materials, but the most basic green strategies owe a lot to old commonsense ways of building, such as placing windows to capture breezes or natural daylight. Though it looks old, this northern California farmhouse is actually brand new, but it does employ timeless techniques that have made some of the best old houses naturally sustainable.

In our air-conditioned modern world, we often forget the simple practicality of placing windows (that you can actually open) on all sides of a house with clear paths for breezes. Set into a hilltop notch, this cross-gabled farmhouse borrows

In the dining room, a favorite chair stands guard between the door to the outdoor terrace (left) and a corridor that leads to the first-floor master bedroom (right).

the lessons and vernacular traditions of American farmhouses. Unlike buildings designed by architects, vernacular buildings reflect a local language and utilize available standard materials. Of necessity simple and built from pattern books or by the ingenuity of local contractors, the farmhouses of the Midwest and West provided simple solutions, such as cross-ventilation in an age before air conditioning, windbreaks for shelter, and front porches for community.

The Best of New and Old As a farmhouse for the 21st century, this house, designed for a young family by Siegel & Strain Architects, combines the best of new and old in sustainable energy strategies and room layout. Sheltered under live oaks, the house is shaded much of the hot California day just as its forebears would have been more than a century ago. Yet, as a new house designed to minimize energy use, walls and windows are well insulated to retain coolness in the day and heat at night, and concrete floors on the main level act as a heat/cool sink. Like many old farmhouses, the floor plan focuses on a central hall and stair with access to a long second floor. On the main level, public rooms open out to outdoor living on the screened porch, the trellis next to the pool, and the shaded front porch.

FIRST FLOOR

→ California casual living is the indoor/outdoor experience from house to terrace to pool. With the hills of Sonoma in the distance, the simple design of the house and landscape takes good advantage of the idyllic potential of this spot. Overhead, a trellis provides a threshold between inside and out.

Borrowing a page from the past, the farmhouse is perfectly suited to simple summer living. Owners Lee and Cathy moved to Sonoma from the city so that their children could enjoy a country life (and go to a good school just down the hill with friends nearby). Life here in the summer is idyllic, and appreciating the beauty every day is a simple pleasure. Indoors is there if you need it, but outdoor living is the joy of Sonoma.

Whether it's for bocce—a favorite local Italian game generally played with a glass of wine in hand—or a swim in the pool, the lawn terrace provides the simple pleasures of casual California recreation. Wet feet running inside for a cool drink leave no marks on the concrete floor. This isn't a wipe-your-feet or take-your-shoes-off kind of place: One of the joys of a simple life here in the countryside is not having to fuss about the house.

Authentic Character This modern farmhouse achieves a sense of place and age not through fake distressed materials or expensive replicas of historic brick and ornament. Rather, an eclectic blend of roof shapes, window types, and wings compresses generations of additions into a single moment. One of the easiest ways to tell whether a farmhouse has been added on to is to look at the roofs. Here, the lower roofs slouch down with a low slope that seems added on so as not to interfere with the upstairs windows.

As a work blending the best of new technology and vernacular traditions, this farmhouse is made of layers of time. For example, in the vernacular tradition, the main-level porch windows are standard double-hung casements. On the second level,

↑ Wood, stainless steel, and white are the palette for the kitchen, with simple industrial light fixtures and a concrete floor completing the picture. The kitchen is separated from the dining room (at right) by a peninsula of cabinets and a change in ceiling height.

→ Furnished with classic modern furniture and a minimalist rug, the living room is an elegant room in a rural setting. The bumped-out bay window pushes the room out into the view down the valley.

→ ↑ The tub in the master bathroom is almost monastic in its simplicity. With towels ready at either end and a view of oak tress framed by the window, it is the epitome of the luxury of enough.

→ → This is the "front" porch view of the house, though in reality this is a 360-degree house without a true front or back. Every room has a view, either a long view down the valley or a more intimate view of the live oaks close at hand.

Simple Solutions What Makes It Sustainable?

In the long term, a building's largest impact on the ecosystem is its energy use for heating and air conditioning. In California, air conditioning is the primary load, so its elimination from this house saved on both the cost of the equipment and the ongoing cost of running it. The simple solution to no air conditioning is built into the house with cross-ventilation, ceiling fans, concrete floors that provide thermal mass to temper the air, insulation that exceeds the building code, and old-growth trees close to the house that provide shade. In all, the result is an efficient, low-maintenance home that has 25 percent to 30 percent lower energy costs than a comparable new home.

four-pane square windows line up under a shed roof. In the "addition-like" wings, single-pane windows are a modern touch that frame hillside views in the kitchen and bathrooms. Despite this complex kit of parts, the house is designed so that it fits together in a simple way that provides a comfortable floor plan inside without looking large outside.

The all-white interior is a dramatic foil for the surrounding forested site with its native grasses and spring wildflowers. Plain white windows frame the grass-covered hillside that wraps the house. White-on-white trim, simple in shape, recalls a farmhouse in a quiet way. Interior wood ceilings are a nod to modern sensibilities, as are the steel stair railings. Galvanized metal is the ceiling finish of choice for the porches and over-hangs, which along with the industrial light fixtures merge new and old, industrial and rural.

Simple for the Long Term It's telling that the first construction project on the site was a tree house for the children. Decorated with a minimal eye, this house has the simple feel of a tree house for adults based on the drama of a few stunning items, such as the enormous antique French clock face that looks out over the central hall. There are corners waiting for just the right heirloom chair. Simple here is not in a rush; the right landmark furniture will show up with time.

This is a house for the long term, with grandfather living in a guest house nearby and a main level that will accommodate owners who want to stay when they are old. Cathy and Lee's commitment to simplifying their lives now is not to wait for retirement to move to the country. Though this makes for some complex commuting, coming home is worth all the trouble.

→ In the front entry hall, steel railings and a concrete floor are modern details within a traditional framework of white walls and trim.
→ → With a whimsical reference to barn building, the upstairs guest room has a sliding door hatch that opens to the stair hall.

By a Factor of 10

A Simple and Sustainable City Home

This bright red townhouse in a Chicago neighborhood shows that a city home can be just as sustainable (and affordable) as a cabin by the shore or a house in the country. The project began when the City of Chicago's Departments of Environment and Housing invited entries for a national competition to design new models for sustainable city houses for the 21st century. Built as one of five winning case studies, this simple city house and its four fellow winners were sold by lottery. Its unusual name, "By a Factor of 10 House," derives from its designer's goal to reduce environmental impacts of energy consumption, materials use, and waste by a factor of 10 over the long term. The lucky new owners of all houses were required to take a class in green design so they would understand the benefits of their innovative homes.

Borrowing from Chicago's row house traditions, this house sets a new sustainable model for city living with a host of energy-saving strategies and an efficient floor plan. Modern in color but traditional in form, the house is a comfortable fit with its neighbors.

The current owner of this house, Thomas (an artist), did not set out to live in a green house, but he enjoys the advantages of living here. It has grown on him, he says, and he now uses environmentally sensitive cleaners, paints, and solvents in his work. As an artist, Thomas likes the simplicity of this house with its high ceilings, open floor plan, and natural light.

Innovative yet traditional, the house is designed to fit its South Side Chicago neighborhood, with its blocks of two- and three-story rowhouses, most of which have a front porch and a front door set a half story above grade. Borrowing from Chicago residential tradition with its predominance of flats stacked up into buildings, this house has a crisp modern look, but it also respects the shape of the older houses in the neighborhood and the character of their siding and awnings.

Inside, the room layout is basic as can be. The first floor is made up of just one large room for living, kitchen, and dining areas. Upstairs, there are three boxy bedrooms just off the stairs. Interior spaces where the daylight doesn't reach are used for storage.

A Chimney of Light and Air The house provides a lot of thrifty comfort in just 1,200 sq. ft. When building small, it makes sense to "borrow" outside views and light from above to amplify the sense of space. For this project, like most rowhouses, getting in light and air are critical challenges because windows are limited to the two narrow front and back ends. Architect Marc L'Italien of EHDD Architecture took this lot's east-west orientation as an opportunity to unify and animate the interior. To light the house all day and to provide passive solar heat, he organized the house vertically around the stairwell or "solar chimney," a vertical space that allows hot air to rise and cool air to sink into lower levels.

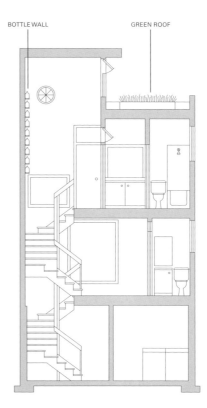

BOTTLE WALL   GREEN ROOF

→ With few interior walls and abundant daylight, the house feels considerably larger than its 1,200 sq. ft. would suggest. Looking over the street, the living room is filled with light from the central stairwell tower.

On winter days, the low angle of the sun shines in the high windows to heat a wall of recycled soda-pop bottles filled with water and mounted high in the shaft. At night, the warmth stored in the bottles radiates into the home, reducing heating costs. At the top of the chimney, fans circulate warm air down in the winter. In summer, Thomas keeps the house closed up during the day. In the evening, he turns on the whole-house fan to blow out the built-up warm air. Then, once the house is vented, he lets in the cooler night air by opening clerestory windows at the top of the solar chimney. This simple vertical space thus doubles as a staircase and a warm-air chimney (or "cool-air waterfall," depending on outdoor conditions) from the roof, and it's far simpler and cheaper to run than elaborate heating and cooling systems.

Thrifty Materials and Natural Light The "By a Factor of 10 House" is an affordable solution for building in the city. Its design involves no superfluous trim work or decorative adornments, and the plan layout uses a cost-saving 24-in. wood framing module to minimize material use. Both inside and out, carefully chosen materials contribute to this home's design and compact comforts. The careful placement of windows maximizes reflected light and reduces glare while allowing for sensible furniture placement. The first-floor flooring consists of cork tiles, a long-lasting and renewable product. The second-floor carpeting is made from recycled plastic bottles.

→ Simply finished with basic materials and built-ins, the neutral background of the dining area becomes a vibrant palette with the changing tones and shadows of daylight.

→ ↑ The center hall is efficient in its small footprint and ability to allow hot air to flow over transoms up to the clerestory windows on the roof.

→ ↓ In the world of roofing options, a "green roof" is surprisingly simple and practical. Thrifty for the owner and the environment, this home's green roof cuts down the need for air conditioning in the rooms below, eliminates storm water runoff, and has a longer service life than many traditional roofs.

Efficient in plan, the simple layout spins off the central stair. The drama of the borrowed light from above spills into the rooms on each floor, balancing the light coming in east and west windows. Borrowing an old-fashioned idea from houses built in the 1900s, before air conditioning, doors leading to the halls on each floor have a hopper window above them that opens to let hot air escape out the windows of the solar chimney. Traditional commonsense solutions for comfort from the era before air conditioning and inoperable windows still work today. This house shows how home designers can make brilliant use of light, air, and space within urban constraints. Whether building in the city or country, creating the simple home means considering the house as a whole, as a working system in which light, air, and spatial design work together for comfort that's affordable and good for the environment too.

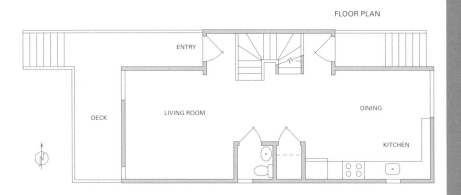

FLOOR PLAN

ENTRY

DECK   LIVING ROOM   DINING

KITCHEN

→ On winter days, the low angle of the sun shines onto a wall of recycled soda bottles filled with water, releasing the stored heat in the evening. This is a thrifty and low-tech approach to reducing energy costs.

Simply Green By a Factor of 10

How much is enough in terms of what each of us can do to be truly sustainable? By one standard of measurement, if we reduce our use of resources by a factor of 10 from current levels of consumption, we will be in balance with the ability of the planet to sustain us all. The By a Factor of 10 House uses four strategies to accomplish that goal:

- Size reduction. At 1,200 sq. ft. (approximately one-third the size of a typical three-bedroom home), the house consumes fewer raw materials, uses less energy, and has less impact on its surroundings.

- Improved energy efficiency. Passive solar gain, "heat sink" (heat storage built into the house), the solar chimney, efficient mechanical equipment, and high-grade insulation all contribute to the energy efficiency of this home.

- Extended lifespan of materials. Built of materials with extended life expectancy, such as cement-board exterior siding and cork flooring, quality prevails over quantity. Product durability will require less replacement throughout the lifetime of the house.

- Impact reduction of products. The framing lumber comes from sustainably managed forests. In terms of indoor air quality, pollutants are minimized by sealed combustion appliances and formaldehyde-free and low-VOC finishes and materials. At the end of its life, this house is designed to be dismantled so it will not end up in a landfill.

Chapter Seven Simple Is Resolved Complexity

Simple Gets to the Essence of Things Seemingly simple things, like maple syrup or a good single-malt scotch, are surprisingly complex to make. Just as it takes 30 gallons of sap to distill out 1 gallon of syrup, the process of designing a simple home is about refining a house down to its essence. What appears low-tech and fairly effortless can in fact represent many decisions and time-tested processes. Such is the case when you try to refine complex family needs into design solutions for a simple home or resolve the complexity of designing a new bathroom. You wonder how you can keep everyone happy, accommodate growing kids, and meet your budget all at the same time.

It's a lot easier to overbuild than to design for refined simplicity. The essence of Zen belief is to arrive at the point in life and design where nothing is unnecessary, and taking anything away would destroy what is there. Any good craftsperson knows that a window without trim is far harder to design and install than one with fancy moldings. A simple window leaves no room for error; it takes special care to finish without the trim that typically covers up the joint between the window and the interior wall finish. Simple design is not elaborate, but it is precise in its proportions and attunement to your needs. The art is in making it look effortless.

In the design of a house, a simple solution looks to all the pieces as a whole instead of trying to fit the bits and pieces together. By contrast, in mass-produced houses, bits of fake ornament are commonly used to cover up mistakes. But simple design strives for refinement rather than ostentation; it is not about masking shortcuts but finding the most direct and lasting solutions to meeting the owners' needs and tastes. And for many modern families, these needs can be complex. They can include accommodating working parents, seasonal storage, and home offices. Designing the simple home means resolving this complexity by looking at the owners' needs as a whole. A less precise solution, as in many large developer houses, is to create a lot of rooms for specialized activities—and label the leftover space a "bonus room." This is not refined design, but an attempt to make unecessary excess a plus.

Distilling Down the Stuff You Need In designing a simple home, a long list of potentially conflicting needs is woven together through compromise and innovative refinement. A good architect can help you see opportunities to pare back on spaces and things you may think you need but really don't. In the design process, you can discover ways to distill many daily actions, such as cooking, baby-sitting, and reading, into one multipurpose space.

Resolving complexity means finding answers to seemingly disparate needs and considerations, such as modern and vernacular, minimalism and comfort, privacy and views. In a house in Tennessee, white gables are both modern and reminiscent of vernacular precedents. On Lopez Island in the Pacific Northwest, small-scale buildings are vernacular in scale and built with modern materials such as corrugated metal. In Minnesota, minimalist modern is livable and comfortable. In Rhode Island, the public rooms are private from the street, and the upper rooms have the big views.

It's easy to seek the salvation of "simple" via decluttering or meditation. But for trend seekers desperately searching for substance, embracing the newest fad will not provide a simple answer. For a family in Tennessee, reducing clutter and wasted space means distilling down a lot of furniture to a few favorite pieces and collections. In a creekside house near Minneapolis, the apparently effortless placement of large windows refines the challenges of indoor daylight with privacy from the neighbors. Here the windows and skylight are so much more than holes cut in walls or ceiling. Rather, they admit great views and daylight and enliven the indoor stucco walls with a wash of light that changes through the day.

Everything should be made as simple as possible, but not simpler.

—Albert Einstein

When it comes to resolving complexity, children have their own challenging set of needs. Kids want to play near the adult action with the result that their toys can be underfoot in the most-used areas. At the creekside house in Minneapolis, the design affords a place for grandkids to spread their out their toys in the living room without creating chaos. For a family on the shore in Rhode Island, refined simplicity creates a home with private escapes for parents and child. The result is a house that feels much bigger inside than it appears from the street. It is respectful of the small scale of its cottage neighbors while offering a rich range of indoor places for family life. No easy task—but it can be done. In the homes to follow, we learn how real complexity can be refined into simple beauty.

The L-Shaped Cottage

A Seaside Haven for Privacy and Togetherness

John and Cheryl hoped to resolve some of life's complexity when they moved from New York City back to Cheryl's seaside hometown of East Greenwich, Rhode Island. With the help of architect James Estes, they built a house that evokes the shingle-style simplicity of the area's early 20th-century cottages with a contemporary sense of spaciousness. They also found a simpler life.

The house is designed for three active people: an artist, her husband, and their young son. The updated cottage serves 21st-century life with a kitchen/dining area that flows into the living room, two bedrooms with baths, and private spaces for each member of the family (a first-floor study for John, the tower studio for Cheryl, and a playroom for their

One of this house's simple beauties is its use of basic materials. Here, the standing-seam metal roof meets the low eave frieze and the shingled wall below in an unselfconscious way.

son). Unlike the cramped cottages of a century ago, where privacy was best found by going out for a walk on the beach, this is a cottage home with indoor retreats set away from each other at the three ends of the L-shaped plan. It is a house of many interior realms and choices for being together or being alone.

Architect Estes wove the house into the neighborhood by using traditional gabled forms in a simple way. With chimney, gable, and long shed roof, the house looks like a set of building blocks spread out on the lawn, almost toylike in its simplicity. The living and study wing faces the street with a corner front door while the longer two-story kitchen/dining wing stretches back toward the edge of a state forest. Looking in from the street, the composition of the façade is simple and clear, with a wall, low eaves that pick up the scale of the neighboring houses, an unadorned living-room chimney rising up from the low-slung roof, and the corner entry porch.

Expansive Views and Private Space This innovative seaside cottage is very much turned in on itself. It has a welcoming entry yet considerable privacy from the street. The narrow footprint of the wings means that the living and dining areas have windows on both sides; they are soaring and open spaces changing with the tonalities of daylight and shadows throughout the day and seasons. The two wings enclose a serene garden room that works as a terrace, backyard, and party space. In the living and dining areas, smaller windows face the street while expansive sets of French doors bring the courtyard inside.

→ The living and dining wings embrace the rear courtyard with floor-to-ceiling glass doors, while the square windows of the bedrooms and tower studio above create their own dynamic rhythm. At ground level, the square lines of the terrace act as extensions of the interior rooms, inviting everyone outside when the weather is warm.

The Best View in the House Sometimes, it makes sense to give the smallest and most intimate rooms the best views. In this case, the second-floor reading alcove perched atop the front porch has a view of the ocean and a nestlike privacy for reading a novel or going online. It's a place where anyone in the family can go for some quiet time. One floor up, the art studio at the top of the tower has an equally expansive outward view, but the downstairs rooms turn inward, focused on the private courtyard in the rear.

Mirroring the L-theme of the house plan, trees and hedges complete the court. Sheltered from the summer sun and winter winds, the courtyard feels safe and protected, in pleasant contrast to the infinity of the ocean views from the upstairs rooms. Behind the terrace and the kitchen/dining wing is the one-car garage. Compatible with the remaining 1920s one-car garages, the structure is visually separated yet close to the main house to help maintain the sense of cottage scale.

Even though the house is inland, it offers strategic views of the water from the second-story reading alcove and the tower studio above. With prime views available only from the upper floors, Cheryl and John chose to put these getaway rooms in the best locations to take advantage of the ocean vistas to the east. Thinking in three dimensions and building upward in the right places, they made the challenge of their site into an opportunity for innovative design and intimate spaces.

Cottage Outside, Modern Inside Presenting itself as a simple cottage to the street and its neighbors, the house feels like a much larger and more open modern home inside. In lieu of traditional cottage moldings and trim, the interior is unadorned and highly functional with strategically located cabinets, storage, and built-in shelving. Approaching the house from the street, the diagonally set glass front entry hints at the modern interior beyond the threshold. Acting as a hinge point for the two wings of the plan, the entry cleverly makes use of the powder room and coat closet as its defining walls. Like the tower studio above,

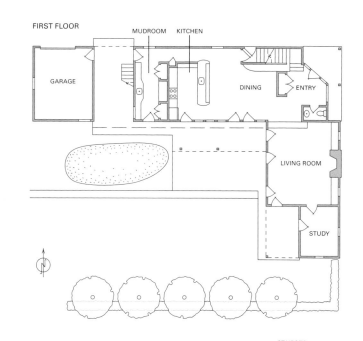

FIRST FLOOR · MUDROOM · KITCHEN · GARAGE · DINING · ENTRY · LIVING ROOM · STUDY

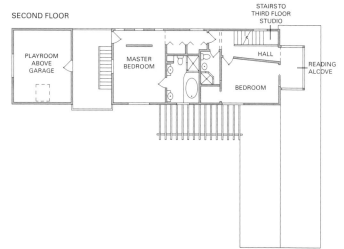

SECOND FLOOR · STAIRS TO THIRD FLOOR STUDIO · PLAYROOM ABOVE GARAGE · MASTER BEDROOM · HALL · READING ALCOVE · BEDROOM

→ By contrast with the traditional cottage exterior, the inside of the house is open and modern. Light floods in along one wall of the kitchen, which is streamlined with brushed stainless-steel, flush-panel cabinet doors, and green slate slabs for counters and backsplash.

→ → The living room is set a few steps down from the entry hall and dining wing, which creates a sense of separation from the other public areas on the first floor. John's study is visible through the open door on the end wall, close enough to the heart of the home yet separate enough for privacy.

the angled entry is a surprising update of the cottage shingle vernacular. And yet, within the greater playful whole, it happily blends in.

Cabinets, doors, and built-ins are defined yet also blend into cottage simple with easily maintained materials, including blond birch, white-painted board ceilings, and white walls, all with little trim and flat surfaces. Plaster walls introduce subtle color variations to highlight the halls and stairway.

With its minimal hallways and efficient layout, the second floor houses the master bedroom and a spare bedroom. A second set of stairs on the exterior leads up to the playroom above the garage and the second-level master-bedroom deck. From the street, you'd hardly know that so many varying rooms and views could ever be housed beyond the quiet and playful façade. Public and private, new and old, this modern cottage shows how harmonious and simple forms can shelter a rich family life.

↑ The simple palette of the downstairs rooms, with neutral tones, blond wood, and white trim, continues upstairs into the master bedroom, which spans the width of the second floor.

↓ At the fireplace and throughout the living room, geometric compositions of windows and built-ins create a framework for contrasts of simple materials, textures, and colors.

→ → Tucked behind the corner closet in the entry hall, the top surface of this dining-room storage unit is in fact a continuation of one of the lower stair treads. Metal hardware accents the basic form and palette of the built-in.

A Simple Compound

It Makes a Village

When you choose an island as a getaway destination, leaving the mainland is part of the experience. The logistics of waiting for the ferry, riding the familiar route through the San Juan Islands in Puget Sound, and then driving down a twisty country road to your home away from home is an opportunity to shift down to a simpler pace. Quality of entry rather than speed of movement is what matters most. If the journey takes some forethought, this island compound of barn, sauna, cookhouse, and studio is strikingly simple—from the square plainness of the studio's façade to the stripped-down rooms of the open barn.

Borrowing lessons of straightforward simple from rural farm buildings, this building houses workspaces for office and studio. At dusk, the building glows with yellow and lavender hues from the curtains on the north-facing windows.

Coming from a fast-paced life in Silicon Valley, Betsy and Peter intentionally sought to create a slower life closer to nature here on Lopez Island in northwest Washington. As they thought about it and discussed it with their architects, Nancy and Joe Greene, their vision became one of less stuff and less architecture. One question they asked: Why build one enormous country house when you can have a rustic village of small buildings, each with its own purpose?

Recalling the old logging camps of the Pacific Northwest and fisherman's villages, Peter and Betsy created a small hamlet nestled in the hillside, clustered around a central clearing, and peeking into Lopez Sound below. The three main buildings are an 18th-century barn moved from Betsy's home in New England, a towerlike studio/office, and a metal cookhouse. At the top of a hill, in an orchard where they are experimenting with fruit varietals, a small sauna and deck provide a retreat in all seasons. The joy of this island life is its natural surroundings, and walking through the woods between buildings is part of the pleasure.

Communal Living Planned for private as well as communal time, the compound accommodates large gatherings of families, offspring, and friends of offspring. In addition to their Red Beach House down by the harbor (featured on pp. 102–109), Betsy and Peter can host visitors in the barn, the studio, the cookhouse, and at campsites up the hill. In a typical summer, their guest book shows that they host more than 125 visitors.

→ The cookhouse is the communal heart of the compound, with places for eating inside and out. Supported by scissor trusses made from Douglas fir trees harvested and milled on site, the interior space is open and airy.

→ → The cookhouse is sheathed and roofed with corrugated metal. Simple in its utility and beauty, it stands in marked contrast to the wood buildings on the compound.

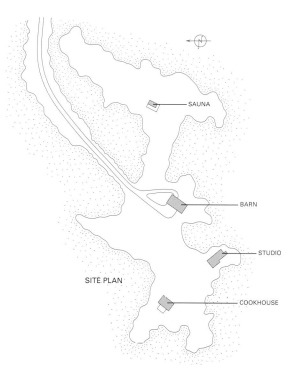

SAUNA

BARN

STUDIO

SITE PLAN

COOKHOUSE

Visitors are often surprised that none of the cottages has a closet. But when you think about it, if you're going to visit a cabin, are closets really necessary? At the beach and the compound up the hill, each small building has a sleepover area with pegs and clothes hooks, a cozy room with reading nooks, and a small wood stove. Guests from the city are awed by the absence of large, elaborate dwelling spaces. Instead, bedrooms are small with large spaces reserved for gathering at the cookhouse or in the office and studio work areas. The joy of being there happens in many simple ways: cooking dinner at the cookhouse using fresh produce from the kitchen garden, collecting alder cones and rocks in the woods, taking a sauna or an outdoor shower at dawn. Guests share meals at the cookhouse, which functions as the heartbeat of the community, but during the day they're on their own, hiking and sailing and enjoying the San Juan Islands.

The Studio in the Forest The forest studio is a no-nonsense building with black concrete floors and well-set-up workspaces that invite creative pursuits. Designed for double duty as an additional guesthouse should the need arise, this is a building with many uses. On the lower level in the back, there is a workout room with views into the forest. In the studio, the easel owns the prime corner; the upstairs office houses Peter's activities and a large flat-screen monitor for group movie presentations. In between is a small kitchen and meeting place for refreshment during the day's projects.

→ In the art studio, a concrete floor and large divided-light windows bring a loftlike feel to the piney north woods. Overhead lights are positioned to illuminate the chosen work spots, not the entire room, while simple curtains can be pulled shut to soften the daylight.

Saving the Best Piece of Land A good rule for building is *not* to place your house at the best part of your site. Rather, save the best views and trees as part of your landscape. Initially, when Betsy and Peter bought the land, they started clearing its highest point with the best harbor views for building. But their architects suggested a site farther down the hill. Today, the original home site is now the orchard and the clearing for the sauna. The mature cedars and alders that huddle around this quiet little clearing are preserved, and the sauna's terrace peeks through the orchard into the marvelous views. It seems right that the best site was saved for the smallest building—the destination you have to make a trek to find.

The mixed siding of cement board and cedar gives texture and interest to the simple structure. With an angled metal roof and industrial-quality exterior sheathing, the studio has a loft or silo-like character with calm interiors and a lighthearted feel. Simple in materials and flexibility, the studio is an easy-to-maintain home for activities ranging from painting to exercise.

Gathering to Dine . . . and to Relax Cooking and dining are the heartbeat of social life at the compound. Peter refers to the cookhouse as the "Temple to Food," and he spends a lot of time there experimenting with recipes. In a climate that permits dinner out on the porch most evenings of the year, it's hard to beat a meal from the kitchen garden overlooking the sound.

The most visible and certainly the oldest building in the compound is the 200-year-old barn relocated from Connecticut, where Betsy grew up. It contains Betsy and Peter's private 600-sq.-ft. apartment and a large communal gathering space with overstuffed chairs and big sliding doors (with no need for screens in this mosquito-free part of the country). To friends used to a different kind of luxury, the joy of lounging in a big comfy chair in a largely empty post-and-beam barn looking straight out into cedar trees comes as a pleasant surprise. This protected openness blends rusticity with the luxury of seclusion, safety, and peace. The experience is very much a conscious choice on Peter and Betsy's part: the quest for the luxury of doing without.

↑ Vegetables, flowers, and herbs flourish in raised beds at the side of the cookhouse. A metal awning above the gable end repeats the overhangs on the front and back of the building.

↓ Originally built in Connecticut, this 18th-century barn was moved here and rebuilt with some modern touches. The large sliding door that used to admit hay wagons now opens into a large open seating area.

→ → The owners have an apartment in the large timber-frame barn. Playing with scale, the large corner window provides an expansive view over the property, while a small punched barn window offers a more intimate peephole to the outside world. The full-length window seat converts to beds for overnight guests.

The Creekside House

Making Life Visible

The simplest houses can reveal the many textures, shades, and prismatic colors of sunlight. No matter the time of year, the play of sun and shadow is the first thing you notice when walking into this well-proportioned, 2,300-sq.-ft. house just 10 minutes from downtown Minneapolis. Medora, the owner, is a former Jungian analyst who holds deep environmental and spiritual interests. Over a two-year period, my architectural firm helped her to shape this house in a process that became a journey of discovery as she tried to simplify and refine her life. The process of building is about making conscious choices that ultimately change you. Focusing one's life on what you really value means resolving the complexity of old habits and attachments, of refining how and where you live down to the finest cognac.

A thick gray stucco wall anchors the right-hand side of the all-in-one main-level room. The wall acts as a light fixture, capturing the sunlight washing down from the skylight above. Surrounding the stairwell is a metal and glass railing, a sculpture in a pool of light.

For years, Medora lived in large city houses near the lakes of Minneapolis. Most recently, she lived nearby in a three-story house set on a hill above the street. The vertical configuration involved a lot of trekking up and down stairs. She often walked with her young grandson around nearby wooded neighborhoods, where the houses were smaller and canopied by oaks and older pines. It was here that she found the third-of-an-acre lot for her new house.

Simple Is Complexity Resolved The creekside house is a study in thoughtful responses to function, daylight, and the steep site. With its plain yellow and gray stucco walls and hardwood floors, the house seems simple both in materials and spatial layout. Yet it grew out of a complex design process that translated Medora's desire for serenity into tangible and specific solutions. From the street, the house presents an elegant and subtle presence of garage, entry door, and small windows. Set close to the curb, the house reflects the scale of the neighbors, yet, as you walk around the side, its broad, flat roofs extend outward as the house steps down the hill. Pennsylvania bluestone walls help tie the house into the hillside and create a sympathetic sculpting of topography.

→ In the compact kitchen, a window at the sink has a view of the woods while the low window at the counter frames a more intimate view. The open cabinet above the counter holds an artful display of the owner's everyday dishes.
→ ↑ Only 16 ft. wide, the living room is cozy enough for an intimate gathering yet open enough to accommodate a busy cocktail party. French doors on the right open the room to the screened porch in summer. The house was intentionally sited to preserve the view of the two large oaks outside the window from above the window seat.
→ → ↑ The back of the house opens up dramatically as it drops down the steep site. Trailing down the hill on the left between two old oak trees, a dry stream bed captures storm water runoff from house and garage roofs and returns it to the ground rather than allowing it to run off into city storm sewers.

Simply Green Start with the Basics

The benefits of sustainable design are not only friendly to the earth, but also to the people who live in the house. Take, for example, the massive stucco walls that nestle this house into the hill while offering protection from the north and west winds. These well-insulated walls are one facet of the energy conservation strategies integrated with this house at all levels of detail. Sustainable design is not an "add-on." In this house, commonsense strategies for solar orientation, storm-water runoff from drives and roofs, and window placement were part of the design process from the start. When thoughtfully integrated with siting and design, such basic building strategies need not require complex mechanical systems or higher costs. Rather, they make use of existing topography, sunlight, and vegetation to optimize the microclimate both inside and out.

As you move inside, there is a sense of cohesion and separation between cooking, dining, and living areas. The 4-ft.-high kitchen counters divide the kitchen from the living room while providing a visual connection at eye level that creates a long view from kitchen to the living room and to the outside. It's amazing that the overall living and dining area is only 16 ft. wide—the width of a double-wide trailer. The addition of a 10-ft.-long, 32-in.-deep bay window in the dining area vastly expands the interior's sense of scale and views to the outside. The overall effect of the windows, the 9-ft. 6-in. ceiling height, and the smooth linearity of the ash floor is an illusion of a surprising vastness that, as Japanese garden designers say, makes use of "borrowed scenery" from the stream valley and surrounding trees.

"What I've learned about myself is how much I love simplicity of function," Medora says of her experience in building. Now, instead of a segmented house of three floors over the street, the new house is "sewn together" by the single stairway, elegantly suspended in space and filled with sunlight. The custom-built steel railing and triangular glass panels catch the sun beaming down from the skylight, with glimpses of prismatic colors along the panels' edges. Throughout the day, the shadows move across the tiger-stripe grain of the floor.

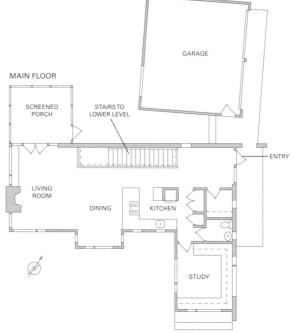

↑ From the street, this new house in an older city neighborhood appears to be one story, which helps it fit the scale of its 1940s neighbors. The gray and yellow stucco-clad exterior is inspired by the color palette of the dry-stone walls on the property.

→ → The custom-stained-glass panel fit into the red front door is a simple way to afford privacy yet still maintain transparency. To the right, the screened porch is visible through the slot between the house and the garage.

Tuning In to the Seasons In Medora's house, there's a sense of connection to the outside without a feeling of overexposure; and this visual link to the outdoors and seasonal change is one way that a small house can feel grand and embracing. As with many seemingly simple outcomes, this sense of protected connection to the outdoors grew out of a conscious and well-detailed design strategy. In all of my design work, I try to ensure that there are sources of natural light from at least two sides of every room. In Medora's office, with its views to the street and a close-by neighbor to the east, long, narrow windows span the tops of the walls, screening out the street and the neighbor and framing views into soaring oak treetops. A large picture window looks south into the streambed.

The effect is a magical one, like being in a grotto overlooking a secret valley, an example of prospect and safe refuge. Yet, throughout the house, the windows are operable so that they can be opened to allow complete flow-through ventilation. They are also divided by horizontal and vertical muntins with a Mondrian-like geometry that is visible but not overpowering.

Simple Is Organized The house features a number of functional storage solutions. The first is the pantry—that seemingly anti-quated kitchen storeroom from Victorian houses that most people still wish they had. The solution: Create a floor-to-ceiling closet just off the hall adjacent to the kitchen. In pantry mode, the tall doors fold open to reveal pull-out shelves for dishes at

→ With the feel of a tree house suspended above the view, the screened porch looks down through the woods to the creek at the bottom of the hill. The floor is bluestone flagstone set in sand for a natural look.

waist height and a band of vertical storage for trays, platters, and other large items across the top. In hall mode, the doors close again as the pantry becomes a hidden room, easily accessible from the kitchen should an emergency fondue pot be needed for extra guests. A second storage gem is the "transit bin" tucked in the entry cloakroom (see the sidebar on the facing page).

A student of American Indian cultures, Medora points out that in the Lakota language there is no word for *art* because art is so much part of life, something integral to the design of tools for living, work, and play. In her new house, the elements of simplicity are equally invisible because they are so grounded in the design at all scales, from the dishwasher (which is raised up 6 in. so you don't have to bend over so far to load and unload dishes) to the grandkids' toy cabinet, built at child height under the serving counter in the dining area.

Ten years ago, when she lived in much larger city houses, such straightforward function might have seemed impossible. Yet people change as they move through their adult lives, and if we think about how we really want to resolve the complexity of our lives, our dwellings can change too. "The house is revealing my life to me," says Medora, "making my life more visible to me every day."

→ A full-height pantry is conveniently located in a hall across from the kitchen. Painted out with the walls, the pantry doors conceal food, pots, and other necessities, leaving the open black ash cabinets in the kitchen uncluttered.

Simple Solutions The Transit Bin

Many of us have bags of recycling, clothes for the charity store, or packages to mail that we intend to take out of the house on a future trip. In the meantime, these articles-in-limbo sit in a corner of the kitchen or, worse, inside the front door for all to see. Rarely do home designers consider the flow of goods in and out of the house as industrial architects must with factories and warehouses. The solution in this house is a "transit bin" in the cloakroom.

Looking a bit like the wooden nooks where schoolkids put their hats and gloves, this storage unit includes several open bays across the bottom suitable for full grocery bags, recycling bins, and portable files. A row of square nooks above accommodates incoming mail, grandchildren's mittens, and other incidentals. Shelves between the top and bottom openings are adjustable to make this a highly flexible storage unit.

Simple Times Seven

Making a Big House Simple

It may seem like a contradiction, but a big house can be a simple house. In the case of this white-on-white Southern home, a big house grew out of seven smaller ones. On a Tennessee hillside, seven gables, the iconic symbol of home, march together with a red front door at their center. Striking as it is, the house is actually made up of the simplest building blocks of home: gables, clapboard siding, minimal trim, and open lawn. There's no imposing two-story arched entry here or brick-veneer façade. What matters are the simple, familiar forms, their details, and repetition at all scales, which give this house its powerful presence.

The red of the herringbone-patterned door is the one splash of color on the exterior of this perfectly symmetrical seven-gabled home. As a counterpoint to the gabled geometry, the front steps rise in a pyramid shape to the front door.

When well proportioned, space can bring simplicity to houses and rooms of all sizes. At 4,300 sq. ft, this three-bedroom house is the largest in the book, but it illustrates many of the best qualities seen in smaller simple homes. Materials are basic and surfaces are flat; rooms serve many purposes. And although the gables spreading out from the front make a big impression, the house is no larger than many contemporary suburban homes.

Paring Down The life lived in this house is a celebration of simple without clutter around. After years of living in a 1950s ranch, the owners hired architect Hugh Newell Jacobsen to create a larger yet simpler house. They had a growing family with two kids and lots of furniture. The usual approach is to move from a smaller home to a larger home so you can accommodate all your stuff. Here, the response was the exact opposite: get more space, but have less stuff. The result is a spare, open, light-filled home built by owners who made a commitment to cutting back on beloved collections, lamps, tables, and couches.

Not all of real life was jettisoned on the way to a simple house. Two boys and all the busyness of a family fit comfortably in this spare home. And Jacobsen did "approve" a few heirloom pieces, including a sugar chest that is now the only piece of furniture in the master bedroom besides end tables, two chairs, and the bed itself. All storage and dressing needs in the master suite are addressed by the built-in storage in the walk-in closet that connects to the master bath.

→ Restful and serene, the master bedroom is spare in its furnishings. In the spirit of paring down, the 19th-century sugar chest, a family heirloom, was one of the few pieces that the owners brought with them from their previous home.

A House without Trim One of the things that gives this house its distinctively simple look is the almost total absence of trim, with no baseboards, few moldings, and very little window and door trim. Ironically, it's harder to frame a window or door without trim than it is with trim, because trim boards can cover up mistakes and rough edges. Without trim, there's no margin for error. The workmanship required to have corners return into recessed window pockets or to eliminate baseboards at the meeting of floor and walls costs more than buying trim to hide problems, but the simple result is dramatic in a way that trim cannot match.

More House with Less Ornament The owners wanted a home that would make a statement, and building pure white symmetrical gables set on an open lawn did the trick. Both modern and traditional, the house is not overly nostalgic with faux columns and complex rooflines. Nor is it starkly modern. Instead, as with all of Jacobsen's work, the design makes bold use of traditional forms: the steeply pitched gables, the mullioned multipaned windows, and slate and wood steps.

As in many simple homes, there are no baseboards, chair rails, or crown moldings to complicate plain walls and ceilings. In the bedrooms, ceilings and doors are 10 ft. high, which makes for a much more vertical sense of scale than in most new construction. In many houses, the ceilings are 8 ft. or 9 ft., and the doors are typically 6 ft. 8 in. The space above the doors blocks visual connection and looks awkward. By spending a bit more money on ceiling height and doors, a much greater sense of space can be created without expanding the overall square footage.

Stepping Up the Hillside As you approach the hillside site, the seven white gables stand directly on the grass without any visible foundations or landscaping. A bright red front door invites you into the village of small houses beyond. Across the threshold, a central hallway organizes the entire house as it gently steps up the hill on four terracelike levels.

The first level houses the small entry hall. The second step up is a single gable that contains the powder room and closet.

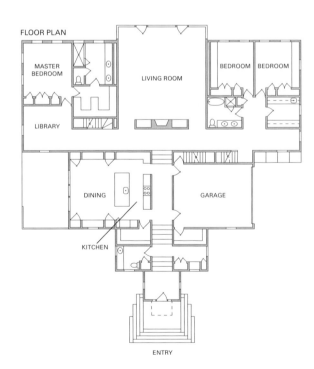

FLOOR PLAN

MASTER BEDROOM

LIBRARY

LIVING ROOM

BEDROOM BEDROOM

DINING

GARAGE

KITCHEN

ENTRY

→ → In the library at one end of the cross-hall, the only break in the wall of books is the fixed nine-pane window. The simple geometry of the window repeats the grid of the bookshelves.

↑ At the opposite end of the hall, a light-filled "room" just off the children's bedrooms is almost monastic in its austerity.

At the third level to the left, the kitchen/dining room is an open space that is a private world unto itself. Cooking and dining are combined in one simple room that, with high-quality finishes used with minimal fuss, manages to be simple and elegant at the same time. Just across the hall, with an easy connection for bringing in the groceries, a garage gable accessible from the side balances the kitchen/dining-room gable. Who would think that such an important space as the kitchen and dining area could pair with a garage? And yet, it's a clever solution to creating direct access from car to kitchen while avoiding the billboard presence of the garage door on the main façade.

The Hilltop Living Room As the seam that holds the house together, the central hall creates a sense of anticipation as you climb toward the top of the house. At the highest level, the central hall and cross halls come together at the living room. With a piano and open seating areas, this glassy pavilion is the perfect place for a large party, with the option for guests to flow outside to the flat rectangular lawn (which was designed to do double duty as a playing field for the kids). A bank of 10-ft.-tall doors and windows opens the room to the lawn and terrace, while the small punched openings in the gable above pick up the repeating theme of the nine-paned windows used throughout the house.

↑ The pleasing balance of symmetry is the power of a repeated simple form. Crisp minimalism in an elegantly simple façade recalls barn imagery with square windows and steep gables.

↓ The stair that climbs the hill and connects the seven pavilions gives a whole new meaning to the term *split level*. Concealed air vents in the openings at the bottom of each stair riser give the impression that the treads are floating.

→ → The thick end wall of the kitchen gable creates deep recesses for the diminutive square windows and accommodates storage and major appliances. With a wall of built-ins and a commodious kitchen island, everything can be stowed away to keep clutter at bay.

The bedrooms are tucked off to the sides of the living room. In the master bedroom, clothes and shoes are stored around the corner, out of sight in the built-in closet. Toothbrushes and other practical necessities are hidden away in cabinets in the elegantly simple master bath with its full-height shower door.

At the other end of the house, the children's bedrooms and bath and the laundry room balance the master bedroom pavilion. Here, symmetry serves the functions of privacy by putting kids' and parents' bedrooms at opposite ends, while allowing for ease of access with a connecting hallway. It's not a forced formality, but rather a balance that seems natural and simple as you move through the various pavilions. Simple does not have to be small. But it does need to be true to its owners' needs and the flow of life in the house. The ordered simplicity in this floor plan accommodates parents and growing children with a sense of effortlessness born from a mastery of balance, proportion, and paring back the clutter that can complicate houses of any size.

→ The vaulted living room is the largest space in the house, made even roomier by the wall of glass that extends the space out into the landscape.
→ → In the master bathroom at the back of the house, sinking the tub below floor level allows space for a full-height window.

Afterword

Now that we have stepped inside a variety of simple homes across the country, you may be wondering how to plan your own simple home. These pages share stories of houses and of how the people who built them took a journey to question what really matters in their lives and environments. Common to all these stories is the wisdom of winnowing down. The San Francisco townhouse that appears in the Simple is Enough chapter could have been opulently large but instead is luxuriously enough with its 900-sq.-ft. living area. In your choices about your home, your own inner balance point is a sufficiency of what you need instead of all that you can attain or afford.

What matters for the simple home is not gadgets, ornament, or the stuff you put in it. Rather a home simplifies and enriches life if it truly helps you to enjoy your own simple pleasures. Thus the first step is to consider what your own pleasures really are, along with a few simple places that you may already enjoy. Perhaps it's your backyard vegetable garden with its neatly tended straight rows or the sense of balance you feel when cleaning and organizing your desk.

Like a beloved garden or creative workplace, simple homes are stages for possibility; they are not overly designed or furnished. Rather they grow and change with the seasons of life. They help us along on our journeys. Simplifying life is not a new-fangled idea. Mark Twain spoke of eliminating "unnecessary necessities" at the height of America's Gilded Age. Then and now, what was most important, what remains necessary, is to find our own inner journeys, not the right set of designs and possessions, but a sense of who we might be.

We can never forecast the future of our lives. But we can begin to choose which paths to take. You know you need somewhere to eat, but do you really need a formal dining room, an eat-in kitchen, and an eating bar? Instead, your house can be one where you can enjoy the scent of a rose through an open window while you brush your teeth, where you can read on a window seat with a view of the back garden, where you can enjoy a bath by candlelight, share a family meal at a communal table, and prepare that meal in a well-lit kitchen. It isn't so much the stuff you put in the house as the way the house allows you to enjoy the simple pleasures of life and celebrate the luxury of your own enough.

How do you know when you get to simple? Simplicity in design and life is not a fixed goal but a mindful path. Like Buddhism and other spiritual paths, the pursuit of honest simplicity is a way of living everyday rather than a religion reserved for special places and times. Finding your own simple home is more than finding the right house; it reflects considered choices for how to live, what to consume, how to be with others, and how to edit out the noise of today's mass media. To help you find your sweet spot, we have suggested six paths that you may follow: simple is enough, simple is flexible, simple is thrifty, simple is timeless, simple is sustainable, and simple is the essence of resolved complexity. You have started down your own path to a simple home by reading this book. Trust yourself, you have unsuspected depths of simplicity ready to come forth.

Architects and Designers

Archaeo Architects
1519 Upper Canyon Road
Santa Fe, NM 87501
(505) 820-7200
www.archaeoarchitects.com
Principal architect: Jon Dick, AIA
The Courtyard House (pp. 152–159)

Barbara Garfield Design
188 Rowayton Avenue
Rowayton, CT 06853
Email: barnwired@aol.com
Principal designer: Barbara Kenworthy Garfield
First Day Cottage
P. O. Box 580
Walpole, NH 03608
(603) 756-3435
Principal designer: David Howard
A Simple Barn (pp. 72–79)

Bouratoglou Architects
303 St. Marks Avenue
Brooklyn, NY 11238
(718) 484-4540
Principal architect: Jill Bouratoglou
Designer and builder: John Bouratoglou
Brooklyn House (pp. 94–101)

CCS Architecture
44 McLea Court
San Francisco, CA 94103
(415) 864-2800
www.ccs-architecture.com
Principal architect: Cass Calder Smith
Simple in the City (pp. 40–47)

EHDD Architecture
500 Treat Avenue, Suite 201
San Francisco, CA 94110
(415) 285-9193
www.ehdd.com
Principal architect: Marc L'Italien, AIA
By a Factor of 10 (pp. 194–201)

EnvironMental Design
1025 Green Lane
Breaux Bridge, LA 70517
(337) 332-6681
Principal architect: Edward J. Cazayoux, AIA
Creole Simple (pp. 134–143)

Environmental Design Group Enterprise (EDGE)
PO Box 2482
Taos, NM 87571
(505) 758.5642
www.edgearchitects.com
Principal architects: Ken Anderson, AIA and Pamela Freund, AIA
Simple in Spirit (pp. 118–125)

Estes Twombly Architects
79 Thames Street
Newport, RI 02840
(401) 846-3336
www.estestwombly.com
Principal architect: James Estes, FAIA
The L-Shaped Cottage (pp. 210–217)

Greene Partners Architecture and Design
2585 Fisherman Bay Road
Lopez Island, WA 98261
(360) 468-3655
www.greenepartners.com
Principal architects: Joe and Nancy Greene
Three Gables Are Just Enough (pp. 102–109)
A Simple Compound (pp. 218–225)

Hottenroth and Joseph Architects
1181 Broadway
New York, NY 10001-7508
(212) 251-0037
Principal architect: Jim Joseph
Down to the Bones (pp. 30–39)

Hugh Newell Jacobsen
2529 P Street NW
Washington, DC 20007
(202) 337-5200
www.hughjacobsen.com
Principal Architect: Hugh Newell Jacobsen, FAIA
Gulf Coast Simple (pp. 160–169)
Simple Times Seven (pp. 236–245)

McMonigal Architects
1224 Marshall Street NE, Suite 400
(612) 331-1244
www.mcmonigal.com
Principal architect: Rosemary McMonigal, AIA
A Farmhouse in the City (pp. 110–117)

The Miller Hull Partnership
71 Columbia Street
Seattle, WA 98104
(206) 682-6837
www.millerhull.com
Principal architect: Robert Hull, FAIA
Timeless Modern (pp. 144–151)

Safdie Rabines Architects
1101 Washington Place
San Diego, CA 92103
(619) 297-6153
www.safdierabines.com
Principal architect: Taal Safdie, AIA
Simple Addition (pp. 80–81)

SALA Architects
326 Hennepin Avenue East, Suite 200
Minneapolis, MN 55414
(612) 379-3037
www.salaarc.com
Principal architect: Paul Buum, AIA
The Stucco-Gabled House (pp. 64–71)

Salmela Architect
630 West Fourth Street
Duluth, MN 55806
(218) 724-7517
www.salmelaarchitecture.com
Principal architect: David Salmela, FAIA
Little White House on the Prairie (pp. 48–57)

Sarah Nettleton Architects
606 Washington Avenue North, Suite 300
Minneapolis, MN 55401
(612) 334-9667
www.sarah-architects. com
Principal architect: Sarah Nettleton, AIA
North Shore Cabin (pp. 178–185)
The Creekside House (pp. 226–235)

Siegel and Strain Architects
1295 59th Street
Emeryville, CA 94608
(510) 547-8092
www.siegelstrain.com
Principal architect: Henry Siegel, FAIA
A Sonoma Farmhouse (pp. 186–193)